INKLINGS

OF

GOD

KURT BRUNER

INKLINGS OF GOD

WHAT EVERY HEART SUSPECTS

GRAND RAPIDS, MICHIGAN 49530 USA

Inklings of God
Copyright © 2003 by Kurt Bruner

Requests for information should be addressed to:
Zondervan, *Grand Rapids, Michigan 49530*

Library of Congress Cataloging-in-Publication Data

Bruner, Kurt D.
    Inklings of God : what every heart suspects / Kurt Bruner.
       p. cm.
    Includes bibliographical references.
    ISBN 0-310-24996-1
      1. Spirituality—Christianity.   2. Bruner, Kurt D.   3. Spiritual biography.
  I. Title.
  BV4501.3.B78 2004
  231'.042—dc22   2003018276

This edition printed on acid-free paper.

All Scripture quotations, unless otherwise indicated, are taken from the *Holy Bible: New International Version*®. NIV®. Copyright © 1973, 1978, 1984 by International Bible Society. Used by permission of Zondervan. All rights reserved.

Published in association with the literary agency of Alive Communications, Inc., 7680 Goddard Street, Suite 200, Colorado Springs, CO 80920.

Interior design by Beth Shagene

Printed in the United States of America

03 04 05 06 07 08 09 /❖ DC/ 10 9 8 7 6 5 4 3 2 1

Contents

PART V: The Religions We Profess

Introduction: A Nagging Suspicion

Man will occasionally stumble over the truth,
but most of the time he will pick himself up and continue on.

WINSTON CHURCHILL

I've seen it in the snowcapped grandeur of the Rocky Mountains and the blood-drenched miracle of my daughter's birth.

I've heard it in the thrill of Beethoven's Fifth and the delight of a giggling child.

I've felt it in the security of my wife's embrace and the grief of my boyhood friend's closing casket.

I've experienced it through a thousand ordinary encounters— and so have you. Clues to a spiritual reality concealed from our eyes but known to our hearts.

Deep within each of us is a nagging suspicion, hints of the God who, try as we might, is impossible to avoid. Even when suppressed, it lingers through the stories we tell, the wonders we create, and the religions we profess. They remind us of that which is written on the tablet of our souls, revealing what the ancient philosopher Socrates esteemed as the unknown God; and what a tenth-century mystic named Francis saw as a halo to the edges of all earthly things.

This book is about that suspicion. It is about an ache in the pit of our souls, and what it suggests. It is about our inklings of God.

7

Religious Isolation

I was born into a family of churchgoers. Like my six siblings, I could recite dozens of Bible stories and Jesus choruses before I could tie my shoes. I look back with gratitude for a mom and dad who cared enough about our spiritual instruction to load us into the station wagon every Sunday, sometimes kicking and screaming, to take us to church. If the panicked routine my wife and I endure with our four kids bears any resemblance, it wasn't easy. But the process paid off. I became a believer. In fact, I became a tiny prophet who boldly proclaimed truth to the pagans around me—creating not a few neighborhood conflicts.

One such incident occurred while walking home from my suburban Detroit grade school, superhero lunch pail in tote. I passed a group of high school boys who seemed to be minding their own business, shooting hoops and drinking soda. But I knew they had to be up to no good. Why? Because they looked cool. You know the type: long hair, bell-bottom jeans, rock music blaring from their eight-track. I had lived in a strict Baptist home long enough to recognize evil when I saw it. And so, in a bold move that showed tremendous courage and folly, I cupped my hands around my mouth and yelled at the top of my lungs, "Sinners!"

The puzzled high school boys looked around to find the source of their condemnation. There I stood, unashamed of my stand for righteousness. They laughed and went back to their wicked schemes, hardly paying me any attention at all. But they made mental note: the little Bruner kid.

Over the next several weeks, those boys retaliated against my entire clan. They did nothing violent or cruel, but they did get even. Whenever members of my family walked, rode, or drove by their home, my outburst haunted us. "Sinners!" they would shout. Of course, this required an explanation from me. Mom and Dad corrected my misguided attempt at evangelism. But the neighborhood boys went on chiding until my fed up father demanded they stop.

That awkward incident sums up much of my experience growing up with faith: confident, in part, due to ignorance. I had no idea what those boys believed. I saw only outward signs that made them different. Maybe they attended a church of another Christian denomination, one that shared the basic tenets of my own. Maybe not. But life in the cocoon of my religious subculture prevented me from looking past obvious differences to any similarities. As I saw it, my church had a corner on the truth—so why bother to examine any others?

Beyond the Cocoon

As a young adult, I began poking my nose out of the cocoon through meaningful relationships with Christians who wore different labels: Methodist, Presbyterian, Episcopal, Charismatic, and Catholic. I discovered similarities I couldn't (or wouldn't) see before. They may have had long hair rather than short, or listened to a priest instead of a preacher, but they clearly worshiped the same God—often more authentically than I.

My seminary years forced yet another step beyond the safety of spiritual isolation. While my studies concentrated on Christian theology, intellectual honesty required a basic understanding of other world religions. There I discovered, unlike the relatively minor disparity between Christian denominations, fundamental differences. Not mere subplot changes, but another story altogether. Billions of people around the world, over two-thirds of the planet, live their lives according to very different religious beliefs. The inevitable questions came. How could so many sincere people be wrong? Even more troubling, might I be wrong?

I realize that asking which faith is right and which is wrong has gone out of style. Skim through the religious section of your local bookstore and you'll encounter an interesting and relatively recent phenomenon. The most popular books on spirituality manage to maintain a polite reverence for all views. Best-selling gurus invite us to glean inspiration from a cacophony of faith traditions, casually hovering over varied religious teachings and texts. Their books make you feel intensely spiritual while maintaining a safe detachment.

Not too long ago, *Life* magazine did a cover story on God. It posed the telling question, "When you think of God, what do you see?" The essay, written by lapsed-Catholic Frank McCourt, has what many would consider an appealing answer. After bringing the reader through a brief overview of the major and minor religious movements in America, McCourt wraps up his tour by saying, "I don't confine myself to the faith of my fathers anymore. All the religions are spread before me, a great spiritual smorgasbord, and I'll help myself, thank you."[1] The problem? He doesn't help himself. Not really. Like so many others, he simply enjoys the aroma of various religious meals without taking their claims seriously enough to eat.

And merely smelling food does not satisfy a truly hungry man.

Don't get me wrong. I would love to believe that all religions say basically the same thing, that all provide different paths to the same destination. But I can't do so and take my own faith seriously. If I believe in everything, I believe in nothing at all.

Call me old-fashioned, but I still accept what philosophers call the law of noncontradiction. Put simply, two ideas that contradict one another can't both be true at the same time and in the same way. Despite the mental gymnastics many use in an attempt to reconcile various religious perspectives, distinct faiths offer very different answers to the same questions. One does not respect any by claiming they all say the same thing. Such a view trivializes rather than unites and demonstrates tremendous ignorance of their distinctive beliefs.

My spiritual journey brought me through and beyond such a silly notion to a more mysterious recognition. I have come to believe that all humanity is on a common quest, striving for answers ultimately expressed through the religions we profess. We are trying to pick the lock of our hearts, hoping to release its unspoken creed.

Muzzled Voice

I am a Christian. That makes me biased. In reality, none of us remain impartial. Whether we willingly admit it or not, we've all adopted some type of indoctrination. Yours may be Christian, like mine. It may be Jewish, Muslim, New Age, or Atheist. But it exists. And the only way to transcend one's prejudice is to openly acknowledge it and thus set aside the illusion of objectivity. I freely admit that I have both smelled the aroma and eaten the food of Christian faith. I do not pretend to view all religions as equally valid. But I have come to view their adherents as equally sincere and equally eager for God. We just use different keys to try opening the same lock.

Actually, it was my religious bias that ultimately forced me beyond the safe haven of my religious cocoon. The apostle Paul, the man who penned over half of the New Testament, shoved me. He did so by articulating the tracks upon which my search for mankind's common creed could run.

In a letter written to his friends in Rome, Paul made a brief but extremely important comment about the human condition. He said that we "push the truth away" from ourselves. Not just truth presented to us, but truth known within us. In his words. . .

> For the truth about God is known to them instinctively. God has put this knowledge in their hearts. From the time the world was created, people have seen the earth and sky and all that God

made. They can clearly see his invisible qualities—his eternal power and divine nature. So they have no excuse whatsoever for not knowing God.[2]

Notice the expressions he uses. "God is known to them instinctively." "God has put this knowledge in their hearts." "They can clearly see his invisible qualities." Paul then explains what we often do with this knowledge:

> Yes, they knew God, but they wouldn't worship him as God or even give him thanks. And they began to think up foolish ideas of what God was like. The result was that their minds became dark and confused.[3]

Every major religious movement claims some sacred text, usually written by the faith's founder or prophets. Jews read the Torah, Christians the Bible, Muslims the Koran. To varying degrees, the faithful of each consider its scriptures authoritative—God's special revelation—the source of answers to life's ultimate questions.

But in an almost scandalous declaration, Paul hints at a different sort of divine revelation, not written in a book, but on the heart. He claims a universal, intuitive knowledge of God—a truth plainly seen—so obvious it must be willingly embraced or willfully suppressed. Thus, the apostle Paul introduces us to the mystery of general revelation . . . the heart's unspoken creed.

Unfortunately, he doesn't say much. Paul barely touches upon the concept, as if it would insult our intelligence to dwell on the obvious.

Maybe I'm slow. Perhaps I've spent so much time examining the trees of special revelation that I missed the forest of general revelation. Dutifully reading my Bible, I neglected to hear the sermon God has been whispering within me (and shouting around me). A sermon, by the way, he also whispers to the other two-thirds of the globe who do not read my sacred text.

At first, such a notion troubled this recovering neighborhood prophet. But if the psalmist rightly says that "the heavens declare the glory of God," doesn't it make sense that the heart would do likewise? And if so, how might we recover its muzzled voice?

The Unknown God

We get a clue from Paul's visit to Athens, Greece—the intellectual capital of his day and ancient home to such philosophical giants as Plato and Aristotle. Athens also served as the world's religious capital, birthplace to a mythological convergence that had come to dominate the Roman Empire.

Paul entered into dialogue with the city's academic elite—those who no doubt prided themselves on cutting-edge thinking and open-minded acceptance. Surrounded by altars celebrating gods from every perspective under the Roman sun, evidence of their religious tolerance literally stared Paul in the face as he presented his own brand of belief. Much like Socrates had done centuries earlier, Paul entered one first-century Starbucks after another to engage in philosophical discourse. Before long, word spread that some Jewish guy from a remote corner of the empire was pushing a new, foreign religion.

"Come and tell us more about this new religion," they said. "You are saying some rather startling things, and we want to know what it's all about."

Keep in mind, discussing the latest ideas is what people in Athens did. Missing the opening of a new philosophy would be as unthinkable as New York critics missing the latest Broadway play. So a crowd quickly gathered to hear Paul make his case.

"Men of Athens, I notice that you are very religious . . ." Paul must have winked as the audience chuckled at such an understatement. ". . . for as I was walking along I saw your many altars."

These "many altars" visibly expressed a view commonly accepted at this time, that every religious myth was equally valid because none were necessarily true in an ultimate sense. Few in the pagan world actually believed their idol to be a deity, especially among the educated class. They saw them as symbols, icons of a greater reality. No one knew which (if any) mythology most accurately reflected the real story of God. They covered their bases, if you will, bringing all religious stories together in one place, hoping their collective script might express a more transcendent tale. But instead of connecting them to the authentically supernatural, they created a culture superstitious in the extreme.

Paul continues. "And one of these altars had this inscription on it—'To an Unknown God.' You have been worshiping him without knowing who he is, and now I wish to tell you about him."

At this point you might have heard a collective gasp of surprise and intrigue. Surprise because few dared claim certain knowledge of the true God, yet intrigued by Paul's piercing insight into their deeper motives.

Why establish an altar "To an Unknown God"? I can think of two reasons. First, weary of trying to keep up with the latest religious fad, exasperated city council members may have wanted to stop the costly proliferation of new construction projects. Enough blasted idols already! But likely a far more substantial reason prompted them to create the unnamed idol. Recognizing their own imperfect knowledge, an altar to the unknown God might better express what all the others tried to say. Like their hero Socrates, the Athenians sensed there had to be a real God out there somewhere, even if his particular name and description remained a mystery. When Paul claimed knowledge of this God, ears perked up.

"He is the God who made the world and everything in it. Since he is Lord of heaven and earth, he doesn't live in man-made temples. . . . He himself gives life and breath to everything, and he satisfies every need there is."

After describing the God of all power, Paul made an amazing statement. "His purpose in all of this was that the nations should seek after God and perhaps feel their way toward him and find him—though he is not far from any of us."

Deep within every man and woman throbs both the desire and capacity to "feel their way toward" the God who, in Paul's words, "is not far from any of us." Yes, there exists a real God our idols only suggest. He wants to be known. He can be known. Everything we are grows out of the fact that we are his offspring. Paul explains further that God can overlook people's former ignorance, inviting them out of mythic shadows into the light of a true story. A story all others are trying to tell. A story that is a myth turned fact by invading history.

Paul concludes his discourse by explaining Jesus' part in that story. Some accepted his message. Others did not. Most wanted to hear more. But all must have walked away from that assembly with eight tiny words ringing in their ears, the same eight words that haunt my spiritual journey today: "He is not far from any of us."

The Heart's Unspoken Creed

If God is not far from any of us; if we all truly are feeling our way toward him—then what are the implications for our journey beyond the cocoon? Let me suggest two.

First, I have no justification for my self-satisfied condemnation of others. While I do not have to accept views that contradict my beliefs, I do have to respect the people who hold them, embracing the profound sense of humility that comes from recognizing God at work within every human soul.

Second, the lock has a specific shape suggested by the pattern of all spiritual quests. We find that pattern not in the answers we give, but in the questions we ask. Not in the food, but in the hunger pangs.

So what is this unspoken creed? What beliefs, specifically, do all human beings share? What mysterious truth is written on the tablet of our souls? In short, it can be expressed in three tenets of the heart—simple yet profoundly significant suspicions that encapsulate our quest. The lock we are trying to pick.

Suspicion One—We Were Made for More

Regardless of religious perspective, every one of us senses that life has to be more than meets the eye. We find contentment difficult to achieve because we know we were made for more. The mundane routine of the daily grind doesn't satisfy that deep, persistent longing within. And it never will.

We create wonders that point to the wonder that created us. We tell stories that suggest a transcendent author. We feel emotions that reflect God's tender heart. But most of all, we yearn for something that seems out of reach.

Maybe we are just dreamers, cowards trying to escape the harsh realities of a senseless world. Or maybe a more compelling explanation exists. What if, rather than trying to escape reality, we are trying to connect with it?

J. R. R. Tolkien said it well. "Why should a man be scorned, if, finding himself in prison, he tries to get out and go home?"[4]

C. S. Lewis said it even better. "If I find in myself a desire that no experience in this world can satisfy, the most probable explanation is that I was made for another world."[5]

Deep down, we know we were made for more.

Suspicion Two—Something Is Wrong

After months of joyous anticipation, little Matthew is born. But something is wrong. He enters the world deaf and mostly blind. Years later, he displays signs of what turns out to be a rare nervous disorder. So begins the difficult life of our now twenty-one-year-old nephew.

A relative newlywed and father of one-year-old Bradley, Don boarded a Phoenix-bound plane a few days before reuniting with his wife and child. He had to get back to the office. Lori and Bradley stayed behind for a second week with family in Detroit. Minutes later, news images flashed across the television screen announcing the crash. A call awoke me that night, informing me that my boyhood pal and best man had died in the flames, along with nearly two hundred others.

A small story buried deep within the midweek paper describes how a four-year-old boy found his father's gun. Lovingly playing with his eighteen-month-old baby sister, he points the "toy" at her and pulls the trigger. The bullet explodes her laughing face. Police say that when they arrived, the weeping boy cried out to his dazed mommy: "It was an accident! I didn't mean to do it!"

Such moments reveal a world that seems cruel and heartless. One need not celebrate many birthdays to know that we live in a broken world. Philosophers call it the problem of evil. For many, it is the primary obstacle to belief in God. We want good but see bad. Best-selling book titles reflect our attempts to reconcile the seeming contradiction.

When Bad Things Happen to Good People
When God Doesn't Make Sense
Where Is God When It Hurts?

"With so much pain in the world," we wonder, "how can anyone believe in a good God?" Simplistic answers do not work. Philosophical explanations do not satisfy. Compassionate sympathy feels nice but fails to remove the heartache. Life hurts and we want it to stop!

Sickness. Suffering. Tyranny. Tragedy. Crime. Cruelty. Depression. Death. They all point to the second reality we all know. Something is wrong.

17

Suspicion Three—It Should Be Made Right

Like the tension of an unresolved musical chord, the wrong of life creates a yearning for resolution within the human heart. Yes, something is wrong. But leaving it there would drive us mad. We must move on to tenet three. We want it to be made right.

Every "once upon a time" requires a "happily ever after," or we leave the story feeling cheated. Every mother's son killed in battle begs for a nation's gratitude to soothe the pain of loss. Every villain seeking destruction demands a hero seeking justice. Every descent into the darkness of depression pleads in silence for a return to the light of joy.

Even while shaking our fist in anger at a God who seems cruel or distant, we reach for a God we hope can set things right and redeem our pain for a greater good. We don't know how. We don't know when. But we know things should not, cannot be left wrong. They must be made right again.

The essence of every spiritual journey is a response to these three suspicions. Our faith, or lack of faith, says something to us about why we exist, what is wrong, and how it can be made right again. So does everyday life—answers bubble up in unexpected places. But are we listening?

Stumbling over Truth

Late for a meeting, I climb the stairway leading to my second floor office. I greet two women on the descent—just before my foot catches the edge of step six. I tumble forward and bang my leg on step eight. I look down accusingly at an innocent stair, portraying the illusion of fault. The women react, asking if I'm hurt. "Fine!" I force a chipper lie, not about to admit that my shin is killing me.

18

"Just a little clumsy, that's all." I scurry off, red faced—wishing no one had seen my moment of embarrassment.

Our stumbles prompt some odd reactions. Why on earth did I get mad at the step? Why did I wish the women hadn't seen it? After all, if I really had been hurt and in need, they would have come in handy. The answer comes down to my pride. I do not like losing control. Even more, I do not like being seen as out of control.

Winston Churchill said that man occasionally stumbles over the truth, but most of the time he will pick himself up and continue on. It is an everyday occurrence. We bump into one of God's messages, confronted and floored by ultimate reality, only to look around to make sure no one was watching. Then we hurry off as if nothing had happened.

We restrain tears during a touching dramatic scene—damming up emotion that might have felt God's heart.

We pretend to follow a conversation miles over our heads—missing an opportunity to learn by concealing ignorance.

We admire the religious conviction of others from a safe distance—respecting sincere belief while resisting the urge to embrace its demands.

Where do such avoidance techniques get us? Further away from the truth we claim to seek.

Might I plead for a little humility, the kind of humility that puts us on the road to sanity? Pride talks; humility listens. Pride postures; humility prostrates. Pride is easy; humility is hard. Let's take the hard road for a moment by admitting that none of us have it all together. None of us possess all the answers. None of us control the universe of our lives. Rather than hurry off, let's pause long enough to reflect upon what we suspect is true: that there is a God who can be known, and that deep down we both crave and dread that knowledge.

I want us to feel our way together along the cracks of life in order to discover the unknown God who constantly drops hints all around us and to explore what our common encounters suggest about our common creed. The hints I'll give grow out of those times I have paused after stumbling—unexpected moments when the heart invites us closer to the God who is "not far from any of us." Each chapter falls into one of five categories: the joys we share; the pain we endure; the wonders we create; the stories we tell; and finally, the religions we profess. I arranged them not according to any system or necessary sequence, but in the same manner I detected them: woven into the fabric of real life.

May the moments we share stir your heart, challenge your mind, and inspire your imagination. I hope they help us to learn to recognize and heed the inklings of God that shout all around us.

PART I

THE JOYS
WE SHARE

Joy is not gush; joy is not jolliness.
Joy is perfect acquiescence in God's will
because the soul delights itself in God Himself.

H. W. WEBB-PEPLOE

CHAPTER ONE

The Divine Comedian

Nyuk, Nyuk, Nyuk.

CURLY

My three sons sit in the backseat as I drive. It is boy's night out—and Dad is taking them to their favorite fast-food restaurant. With a wad of cash in my pocket, the fun account looks full and ready to draw down.

"Do I have to order a kid's meal?" asks Kyle—my oldest, skinny as a rail despite eating like a rhino. "Or can I get a double cheeseburger?"

What the heck! I figure we can live on the wild side, for once.

"Sortney!" I say in my best Curly voice from the Three Stooges. (Translated: "Certainly," for my female readers.) Having amused myself with such a believable impersonation, I go even further, mimicking the high-pitched, prolonged falsetto sound— "wububububub"—Curly made whenever fleeing a scene. (Translated: "Let's get outta here!") On a roll, I put the icing on the cake by squeezing a pronounced "Nyuk, nyuk, nyuk!" out one side of my mouth. (No English equivalent available.)

Chuckling at myself, I peer through the rearview mirror to catch a glimpse of what I expect to be laughing children, justifiably proud of their comedic father. "You're the greatest Dad! No one can do the Three Stooges like you!"

That's what I expect to hear. Instead, I see blank stares. Actually, embarrassed stares. Finally, Kyle speaks. "Um, Dad—what are you doing?"

At that moment, I realized that I had failed my children. Somehow, my boys had lived on this earth for nearly a decade without experiencing the infamous Three Stooges, the greatest guy-humor act in human history.

"Do you mean to tell me you've never seen the Three Stooges?" I ask, dumbfounded.

"The three what?" asks Shaun, my second born (second deprived boy).

"Oh my goodness!" I scream, the solution already forming in my mind. "Boys, right after we eat, I am taking you to Blockbuster Video."

And so I did. I rented several Three Stooges tapes and rushed home to introduce my sons to Larry, Moe, Curly, Shemp, and Joe. I took time to explain each character, the main plotline of every episode (which took all of ten seconds), and that all true Stooge fans recognize Curly as the best of the bunch.

My wife, Olivia, watched in perplexed horror. Moms have never understood what guys see in the Stooges. She worried that her kindhearted angels would start bonking one another on the head and poking each other's eyes. I calmed her fears, explaining that no boy should grow up without the enrichment of Stooge humor— and that I would instruct our sons in the strict safety rules of Stooge imitation. She just shook her head and walked out of the room.

Over the coming months, I introduced my boys to several other great acts, including Abbott and Costello, the Marx Brothers, the Little Rascals, and of course, *Gilligan's Island*. Before you knew it, I could imitate almost any great comedic act while driving, and my boys could immediately recognize the source. I had restored my good-dad status!

Be it slapstick like the Stooges or a slightly more sophisticated sitcom like *Seinfeld,* humor is a wonderful gift. And whether prompted by a stand-up comedian or a child's misspeak, laughter feels good.

I figure God must have a wonderful sense of humor. After all, he could have made passing gas an entirely silent activity. Instead, he set up every dad, uncle, and grandpa for the "pull my finger" trick, prompting childhood giggles since the beginning of time.

My Grandpa Grey loved a good laugh. A retired truck driver, he had a rough look with a gentle temperament—kind of a cross between John Wayne and Jimmy Stewart. He and Grandma lived in a small house about a mile from ours. I remember riding my bike to their place nearly every day one summer to help Grandpa work on lawn mowers, something he did in retirement to earn extra cash. I was only about ten years old, so I probably got more in the way than anything. Still, I felt like I was doing something.

One day, Grandpa's mischievous side got the best of him—and me. For some reason, he needed to shorten a particular bolt to better fit the mower he was fixing. So, using his hacksaw, Grandpa cut it down to size. I watched as the friction of metal on metal cut through and eventually released the quarter inch of excess bolt, causing it to fall to the ground. "Quick, hand me that piece," ordered Grandpa.

Naïve to the dynamics of metal friction, I dutifully obeyed, glad to finally be of some use. A split second later, I felt the smart of burning flesh, threw the hot metal piece up in the air and yelled out in pain. Just as quickly, I tried to regain my composure as if it had been no big deal, hoping to preserve my façade of manhood.

Nearly forty years later, I can still hear my late grandpa's uncontrolled laughter. The wheezing chuckle lasted for some time in his smoker's throat and would start all over again when he relayed the story to Grandma and my parents. Admittedly, at first I didn't think it was funny. But it is now one of my favorite Grandpa Grey memories, one that prompts an occasional chuckle of my own.

What made that moment so funny? How did burning a kid's hand prompt laughter rather than outrage? Why do I look back at the incident with fond rather than angry recollection? I believe it has something to do with the nature of humor and the deep well of joy it taps.

Laughter is a funny thing. It catches us by surprise, sneaks up, and overtakes our composure when we most want it maintained. Have you ever tried to suppress a laugh in church when something strikes your fancy? It can't be done without severe damage to vital internal organs. Or how about the time you found yourself in the middle of a big marital spat, determined not to back down first. Suddenly, for some strange reason, your funny bone got tickled. An odd comment or look made the entire battle seem silly. You reluctantly giggled, making your spouse laugh too. The tension dissipated, and before you knew it, you were making passionate love to one another. The moment, and maybe the marriage, was saved.

Great comedy is mysteriously wed to surprise. Someone does the unexpected and it makes you laugh. It may be Moe bonking Curly on the head, Robin Williams acting nutty in a most inappropriate setting, or an unsuspecting child eagerly retrieving a hot bolt. It could be the sudden rush of happiness that comes when all hope seems lost but surprise overtakes the moment. Do you remember the scene in *The Sound of Music* when pursuing Nazis find it impossible to start their cars, even as two nuns confess to their Reverend Mother the sin of stealing engine parts? Their unexpected action saves the day—so we laugh, both at the humor of the moment and the relieved assurance that our heroes will indeed escape. The surprise of both prompts a deeply satisfying laughter and suggests the true comedy others merely echo.

Sudden eruptions of laughter are like tiny sparks bursting forth from a mighty bonfire called joy—a blazing flame that finds its source in a joyous God.

Shortly before his death in 1321, a man named Dante Alighieri completed an epic poem destined to become the most influential work of its type ever penned. Written over a nearly twenty-five-year period, his three volumes eventually were compiled into a single work known as *The Divine Comedy*. This medieval masterpiece of Catholic imagination chronicles Dante's journey through the hell of Inferno, the purification of Purgatory, and the ultimate joy of Paradise.

Those who have read Dante might wonder why anyone would ever call it a comedy. There are no jokes. And while I suppose some of the humor might get lost in translation from the original Italian, few scenes draw even a smile, let alone laughter. Dante purposefully chose the word *comedy* in contrast to the word *tragedy*. His story, like his theology, has a happy ending after a dreadful beginning. The pain of bad eventually gets overtaken by the surprise of good. The laughter comes not in response to slapstick humor but in response to unspeakable joy—the misery of human failure undone by the cheer of divine redemption. In short, the true bonfire of delight, made even more delightful by the temporary sorrows we endure.

Without God, the story of life is, by definition, tragedy. Without a divine comedian, we have no one to write in the surprise of joy. Oh sure, we can manufacture the cynical laugh of satire or the sick joke of cruelty, as children mercilessly tease the outcast. But such attempts at laughter feel empty at best, warped at worst. They fail to scratch our itch for happiness, and dim rather than reflect the divine spark within every man. The truly great comic remains both positive and wholesome. Laugh with Bill Cosby and you feel refreshed. Laugh with Eddie Murphy and you feel ashamed.

Dante, like the Stooges and Grandpa Grey, remind me that we are not meant to take our current experience too seriously. Yes, we may suffer the inferno today, but the surprise of paradise is yet to come. A comedian writes the story of reality. He can use serious scenes as a setup for unexpected laughter. The darker our days, the more we yearn to laugh—not in order to escape reality, but to connect with it.

God is not a cruel prankster enjoying our pain, but a truly gifted comedian, one who delights in our happiness. He does not laugh at us. He laughs with us.

INKLING

WE LAUGH BECAUSE GOD IS DELIGHTFUL.

CHAPTER TWO

The Happiest Place on Earth

I lived only during those times when I believed in God.

LEO TOLSTOY

We roll along in the van approaching the Disneyland gate. Everyone feels excited—and a bit anxious. Kyle and Shaun, our older boys, see Thunder Mountain. Their stomachs tense with the knowledge that this year both can ride.

At four, Troy feels nervous about running into Mickey or some other character. He knows they walk around the park greeting children, a prospect that has given him nightmares. It is one thing to enjoy their shenanigans on screen. But to come face-to-face with a giant Goofy? Scary! "Don't worry Troy," we reassure. "We'll tell them to stay away from you."

Nicole is eighteen months, but even she feels excitement in the air.

I reach the parking attendant and pull out my wallet to fork over the first of many bills to be spent this day—the start of my own anxiety. Meanwhile, Olivia begins her instructions to the children. She knows what to expect and wants to head off problems at the pass.

To Troy: "Remember, some of the lines will be long, so you'll need to be patient."

To the older boys: "We'll be going back and forth between big kid and little kid rides, so no complaining."

To everyone: "You can each have one sweet snack, so choose wisely."

And most important of all: "I don't want to hear any whining today."

Yeah, right! As if that one ever works. Still, warning children helps to minimize offenses. Or so we like to believe.

The day goes pretty much as you might expect. Lots of fun mixed with impatient line waiting, complaints about the kiddy rides, incessant whining, and too many sweets.

Disneyland calls itself "the happiest place on earth." That's its goal. That's its image. Just watch the commercials—always a cute, balloon holding, happy toddler hugging Mickey Mouse on Main Street. You never see a hot, whining four-year-old running for his life from Goofy.

Still, Disney does pretty well fulfilling its motto. But I am convinced that it is not so much going to Disneyland that creates happiness as anticipating and remembering Disneyland.

The weeks approaching our Disneyland trip? Terrific. Kids on their best behavior in response to Dad's empty threats to cancel the trip if chores weren't done and attitudes checked. Nighttime dreams filled with the sights, sounds, and smells of the Magic Kingdom. Daytime conversation packed with attraction descriptions and character imitations. It seems that the longer we looked forward to the day, the more happiness we squeezed out of the experience.

And the weeks, months, and years following the trip? Also great. Our camcorder tape and photo stills remind us of the fun. Our memory banks recall the best moments of the day and seem to edit out the bad scenes (or enable us to finally laugh at them). Troy forgets the panic. Mom forgets the whining. Even I forget the cost. Looking back, we all see it as a perfect day.

It's often that way in life. The file cabinet of our minds places happy memories and fond reflections on top and in front while hiding the unpleasant in a remote bottom drawer. Sure, we can find them if absolutely necessary. But who wants to?

Alexander Gordon's life has been anything but fun and games. As a boy he fled his homeland because of Jew-hating Nazis. Officials forced Alexander to leave his family to live with strangers of a different culture and language as one of thousands of Jewish child refugees taken from their parents and sent to England on the "Kindertransport." Adding insult to injury, British authorities later arrested him, along with other teenagers with German accents. These "enemy aliens" were shipped to Australia to be interned for the duration of the war. While recalling the horrible conditions of his journey and his roaring hunger, Alexander pauses, realizing that such painful memories do not define his life. In his words, "The good thing about life is that you remember all the good things that happen to you, and bad things, you forget about them and you have to make an effort to really remember them."[6]

While enduring the torture of labor pains, my wife wonders why she ever allowed me to touch her. Five minutes after birth, however, she knows only the joyful tears of new life.

I fondly remember the moment I walked across the stage to receive my college degree. I forget about the boring lectures, textbook readings, and term paper deadlines.

I can still see the breathtaking beauty of my honeymoon bride. I scarcely recall our cheap honeymoon hotel or awkward honeymoon inexperience.

It would be just as easy to remember only the bad; many people do. But the deeper desire for happiness overtakes my memories of frustration, regret, and pessimism. Why is that? Does the tendency to remember happy times and forget frustration suggest emotional health or mental illness? Is it a benefit or a defect, an antiseptic or an antidote? Am I reaching for happiness out of self-deception or self-discovery?

I suppose it depends upon whether you believe we were made to smile or made to frown.

~◎~

It is difficult to pinpoint the exact moment happiness occurs. In fact, I'm not sure we can. Like love or gratitude, we experience happiness apart from a particular time or place. Circumstance neither triggers nor constrains it. It is more spiritual than emotional. And like the best gifts, it often arrives when least expected.

For Count Pierre Bezukhov in Leo Tolstoy's *War and Peace,* the gift showed up while he suffered as a prisoner of war. An heir to great wealth, Pierre had lived in the lap of Russian luxury since childhood. He had known the prestige of titled position. But he could not find the contented happiness he desired. Marrying the most beautiful woman in Moscow brought only the shame and misery of her infidelity. Religion infused some meaning into his life but did not arouse lasting joy. The heroics of battling tyranny brought temporary excitement but not happiness. And then, in the least likely situation, happiness rested upon him like a butterfly gently landing upon an unsuspecting shoulder.

Bezukhov's captors forced him to trek hundreds of miles across the frozen Russian countryside behind Napoleon's retreating army. Bitterly cold, hungry, perhaps doomed to hang, Pierre suddenly encountered the elusive happiness he had sought. All pretense had been stripped away. With no real hope of escape to the life he once knew, he began to reflect upon the true nature of life and the reality of God. In the words of Tolstoy . . .

> The gratification of desires—good food, cleanliness, independence—now that he was deprived of them all, seemed to Pierre perfect happiness. . . . All Pierre's thoughts of the future

were directed toward the time when he would be free. But nevertheless, afterwards, and all his life long, Pierre thought and spoke with enthusiasm of that month of imprisonment, of those strong and pleasurable sensations which would never return again, and above all of that utter spiritual peace, of that perfect inward freedom, which he had experienced only at that time.[7]

In many ways, the fictional experience of Pierre Bezukhov reflects the true-life experience of his creator. In his autobiographical book, *A Confession,* Tolstoy describes his own pursuit of life's intoxicating diversions—fame, wealth, influence—only to face the cold stare of emptiness. And yet, refusing ultimate despair, an insatiable lust for happiness drove him on.

> I stopped and looked at myself and at what was going on inside me. I recalled the hundreds of occasions when life had died within me only to be reborn. I remembered that I lived only during those times when I believed in God. Then, as now, I said to myself: I have only to believe in God in order to live. I have only to disbelieve in Him, or to forget Him, in order to die. What are these deaths and rebirths? It is clear that I do not live when I lose belief in God's existence, and I should have killed myself long ago, were it not for a dim hope of finding Him. What then is it you are seeking? A voice exclaimed inside me. There He is! He, without whom it is impossible to live. To know God and to live are one and the same thing. God is life.[8]

Tolstoy's epic novel and personal journey reflect the same reality. We desire happiness because we feel homesick. Tolstoy's heart, like all hearts, encountered its unspoken creed: We were made for more. We were made to be happy because we were made to know God. When we encounter happiness, however brief, we catch a glimpse of someone we have never seen, but miss nonetheless.

So why all the unhappiness? Why do the sick and poor suffer misery while the rich and famous commit suicide? The second suspicion of the heart helps us to understand: Something is wrong. The grain of life runs against that for which we were made.

When times go bad, we easily lose faith in God. We expect better from him. God is supposed to swat away the flies of pain. If he doesn't, why believe?

And then the good times come, distracting us from God with every possible amusement. My favorite T-shirt slogan reads, "So many books, so little time." Who can fit spiritual matters into a busy schedule with so much work to do, so many games to play? Unfortunately, like every wrong turn, the further we drive, the more ground we lose.

Still, nothing can change the simple reality that we long for joy. We long to go home. Circumstances cannot steal from the truly happy or give to the truly miserable. Neither depends upon their proximity to pleasure or health or money. They depend rather upon their proximity to God.

Of course, it would be silly to suggest that only the religious experience happiness. I've met too many happy unbelievers to think that. Moments of joy, like drops of rain, will fall on the religious and the atheist farmer alike. But the refreshment of water and the lift of a smile have the same source. Without God, crops die and faces frown.

Smiles provide much-needed reminders that we were made for happiness, like sips of a drink we long to guzzle. Sure, they fall far short of the reality we desire. But they won't let us forget that we were made for something more. Something even better than Disneyland.

Thank God!

INKLING

GOD MADE US FOR HAPPINESS.

CHAPTER THREE

Nothing Like It

With my body, I thee worship.

BOOK OF COMMON PRAYER

My wife, Olivia, and I lie next to one another in bed, on our backs gazing at the ceiling, or perhaps propped against our pillows in Mike and Carol Brady fashion. Moments earlier, we made passionate love. In the movies, we would be lighting up a smoke. But this is real life, so we are likely to be holding hands or caressing arms while talking, or reading, or crying.

The day may have been spent away from the kids, celebrating our anniversary with relaxed conversation and a romantic dinner out. Or it may have been spent resolving business conflicts, wiping runny noses, sending urgent emails, changing dirty diapers, and fixing broken bicycle chains. Rested from the former or exhausted from the latter makes little difference. The love, attraction, and physical urges that trigger intimacy caused one of us to make the first move—and the other willingly followed.

Sometimes it happens because we both feel an overwhelming sense of love for the other. We act on an unselfish desire to please. Other times it happens because one of us feels stressed or frustrated or insecure, and we need to be pleased. Other triggers also come into play: a romantic movie, a playful mood, the hope of a child, or an innocent touch. While the causes vary, the effect remains as wonderful as ever.

Sexual intimacy is a very private experience. The reasons and ways Olivia and I enjoy one another remain uniquely ours. The frequency may approximate others. The likelihood of mutual satisfaction may statistically reflect the population at large. We don't know. We don't care to know. You see, despite billions of couples making love, none of them are like us, no matter how similar their experiences may seem. That is the wonder of physical intimacy. God gave a gift called sex to all men and women, but it can be truly known only between one man and one woman.

When my oldest son Kyle turned eleven, I felt I should ease into a conversation about sex. I planned to tackle the topic in two phases, starting with the forty-thousand-foot view. I told him that we were going out for video game fun and an important talk during dinner. I figured he would respond with his usual enthusiasm over a father/son activity. Instead, he responded with suspicion. Maybe my tone of voice or the nervous perspiration rolling down my face gave it away, but he sensed a setup—like the times we took him to see "the nice doctor," who ended up giving him a shot. Kyle felt excited about the video game portion of the outing but forced me to tip my hand on the other. The interrogation began.

"What is the 'important talk' about?"

"I think it is time for me to explain where babies come from," I responded.

"Dad, do we have to? I'm only eleven years old! Besides, I already know."

"How do you already know?"

"Alex told me."

Drat! Preempted by his eleven-year-old buddy. It appeared my son had forced me into damage control mode. "Well, I want to make sure what you've heard is accurate," I retorted.

"Don't worry, Dad. *Alex knows!* His dad told him."

I wasn't sure whether to feel relieved or more concerned.

"Well, it is still important for us to talk about it. Besides, we'll have a great time!" I said firmly. So we scheduled our day and made our plans. Kyle chose the video game outlet and restaurant. I outlined the talk—and away we went.

After several dozen rounds with the Jurassic Park video battle against dinosaurs—costing me more quarters than I had planned to spend, but a brilliant delay tactic on my part—we headed off to chat over a burger and shake. I took a deep breath and dove into my explanation, trying to respect Kyle's claim to already know this stuff.

I didn't realize how awkward and embarrassing it would feel to tell my son what I did to his mother in order to spawn him and his siblings. I mean, to those outside the experience, it really does sound like some sort of cruel torture. But I got through my speech and felt good that, regardless of what Alex had said, my son now had the basic facts of life.

But how to interpret that moment of awkward silence and the odd stare?

"Well," I broke the tension, "did Alex know? Is it like what you thought?"

"Dad," a slightly nauseated Kyle responded. "It's nothing like what I thought!"

Relieved and enlightened, we changed the subject and finished our meal.

Nothing like what I thought. Those very words sum up my experience with sexual intimacy—the reality far different than the pornography-informed adolescent assumptions residing in my mind. It is so much more beautiful, exciting, and—at times—routine. Olivia and I have enjoyed intensely pleasurable moments that thrilled us beyond expression. We have also enjoyed times more comfortable and relaxed, like wearing warm slippers on a cold morning. All of it wonderful—but none of it like what I thought.

✦

Traditional wedding vows used to include the line, "With my body I thee worship" as an apt intimation of marital sex. I don't know why the phrase was removed. Nothing better describes the reality or says as much about our spiritual selves. Be it the most intense bedroom frolic or the tender thrill of holding hands, the joys of physical intimacy suggest a spiritual reality much more wonderful than can be perceived and far more satisfying than can be imagined.

In our greatest sexual moments, Olivia and I merely touch round the edges of an intimacy we were made to know. We are like children playing in a sandbox, eager for the ocean beach. What we have is great; what we will have, infinitely more satisfying. Today we worship one another with our bodies. Someday, we will worship our Maker with our whole beings. And it will be nothing like we thought.

Sadly, many of us have drawn distasteful pictures of human sexuality. We have made it all about individual gratification, expressed in our pornography and culture of casual sex. When it becomes about me, others exist to satisfy my whims, be they *Playboy* nudes, streetwalking prostitutes, or abused children. Pregnancy becomes an accidental and dispensable consequence rather than an anticipated and desired blessing. The thought of God is the last thing we want invading our sexual thoughts. We become trapped in a self-consumed cycle C. S. Lewis described as "an ever increasing desire for an ever diminishing satisfaction."[9] An ugly image indeed.

Others have made procreation the sole purpose of sex, rather than its joyous reward. For them it becomes a necessary evil, a guilt-inducing embarrassment, or a wicked indulgence. God could have made human sexuality more like that of animals, giving us the urge only around females in heat. Children could be conceived while keeping desire and pleasure to a minimum. Or sex could have been a sweet and loving experience without the hassle of erotic urges. This certainly would have eliminated the abuses of premarital fornication, extramarital adultery, and email porn ads. But for some reason, God made sex intensely pleasurable. He made it something we can't help desiring or stop pursuing. He made it something we can choose to enjoy either within the healthy parameters of fidelity or as disease-ridden obsessions.

At its best, sex is about intimacy between two individuals, each trying to please the other. Personal gratification is a gift received, not an entitlement taken.

At its best, sex is a very private experience within the security of an exclusive relationship. Despite our ravings to the contrary, we all long for that ideal: one man with one woman, enjoying faithful intimacy in all its forms, for a lifetime.

At its best, sex gives and receives guilt-free pleasure within the parameters of marital fidelity. Expressions outside that protective fence become physically, emotionally, and spiritually reckless, with potentially deadly consequences.

At its best, sex tells me something about God. It tells me he created intimacy as a reflection of his passionate heart. It tells me he longs to please us and be pleased in return. Perhaps most importantly, it tells me he expects exclusivity. When I said yes to Olivia, by extension I said no to all other women. In similar manner, God deserves my fidelity. Intimacy with God, like sex with my wife, is an intensely private experience. It is a gift both given and received.

In 1995, Olivia and I took a week in Maui to celebrate our tenth wedding anniversary. With two preschool children at home, it had been years since we spent more than a few days alone together. We had a wonderful time enjoying the warmth, scenery, food, reef diving, and whale watching. But mostly, we enjoyed one another—feasting on love, creating some of the highlights of our now eighteen-year sexual relationship.

I will never forget the evening of our last day. Olivia was reading in our oceanfront hotel while I sat reflecting on the rocky shore. Waves crashed against the beach as the sun slowly set in the distance. As I sat listening to the ocean, feeling the warm breeze and gazing at the orange horizon glow, I felt as if something spiritual were taking place. I felt as if a lover, The Lover, were gently caressing my spirit, inviting me into an intimacy much like, but very different from, that which Olivia and I had been enjoying. This was not sexual, but rather, a greater reality that sex can merely suggest. I have felt similar sensations when reading a stirring book, playing with my laughing child, or holding my wife's hand.

At such times I know that God makes the first move and invites me to willingly follow.

INKLING

GOD SEEKS AND OFFERS INTIMACY.

CHAPTER FOUR

Beautiful

There is one kind of beauty of the spirit
and another of the body.

St. Thomas Aquinas

Both died the same week in 1997.
Both were included in *Time* magazine's list of the hundred most significant people of the twentieth century. And both were beautiful.
For years it seemed nearly impossible to miss her face. It appeared everywhere—on television, the Internet, the cover of *People,* and every fashion magazine known to woman. If you stood in a grocery store checkout line, you would encounter tidbits or lies about her splattered all over the tabloids. Her life, or at least how fans perceived her life, became an open book. Her image, or at least how the camera captured her image, earned universal recognition. As *Time* magazine described her . . .

Diana was beautiful, in a fresh-faced, English, outdoors-girl kind of way. She used her big blue eyes to their fullest advantage, melting the hearts of men and women through an expression of complete vulnerability. Diana's eyes, like those of Marilyn Monroe, contained an appeal directed not to any individual but to the world.[10]

Diana was a part of my generation, a child of the early 1960s. By the time she turned twenty, already she had graced the cover of

Time magazine—not because of anything she did but because of something she was. The moment Diana said yes to Prince Charles, the shy, pretty girl he admired became the glamorous princess we adored. She entered the world of royalty, fulfilling the fairy tale dreams of little girls.

No matter what you thought of Princess Diana's persona, you couldn't deny her beauty. It seemed similar to yet different from other glamour icons. She was not a sex goddess, though possessed a subtle sensuous allure. She had a lovely figure, but her face drew you before her body did. Other women used suggestive clothing and positions to turn heads. Diana didn't need to. She wore an elegant, sophisticated beauty, not the diminishing kind put on by taking it off.

She died tragically by any definition. Only thirty-six years after her birth and sixteen after her first *Time* cover, Diana's lovely body lay twisted and battered with her limousine after a car crash caused by—of all things—her chauffeur driving irresponsibly a hundred miles per hour to outrun a photographer who was trying to snap yet another picture. On August 31, 1997, her beckoning blue eyes closed for the last time—a victim, in a sense, of her own famous beauty.

Five days later, the world lost another icon. Unlike Diana, however, this woman never graced the cover of a single glamour magazine. She possessed a different kind of beauty, the kind that comes from doing rather than looking good.

Agnes Gonxha Bojaxhiu was born to Albanian parents in 1910 amid intense ethnic hatred. At seven, murderers took her father. At eighteen, she emigrated to Ireland and joined a convent. Three years later she began teaching at a girls' school in India, a position she left to live and work among the poor and terminally ill of Calcutta. In her words, she felt called to "follow Christ into the slums," ghettos created by a particular religious system. Hindus believe in reincarnation and the law of karma. If you have a good life, it is because you did well in your prior life. If life is tough, it is because you have debts to pay from past life wrongs. Helping those in pain serves only to prolong their repayment plan—so it doesn't happen.

Mother Teresa, as she became known, had a different view. She believed that the law of love compels us to help those in need and to comfort those who suffer. The "something wrong" in her theology was not karmic debt but fallen humanity.

Bharati Mukherjee, a Calcuttan woman who observed Teresa caring for lepers, felt puzzled and suspicious. What was this Catholic nun's real motive? Was she covertly trying to proselytize Hindu children? Or was she just an idealist?

"Lepers were a common sight all over India and in every part of Calcutta," recalls Mukherjee,

> but extending help beyond dropping a coin or two into their rag-wrapped stumps was not. . . . The ultimate terror the city held had nothing to do with violence. It was fear of the Other, the poor, the dying. . . . And so I could no longer be cynical about her motives. She wasn't just another Christian proselytizer. Her care of lepers changed the mind of many Calcuttans. Young physicians, one of them the uncle of a classmate, began to sign up as volunteers. It all made Mother Teresa seem less remote.[11]

Decades of self-sacrificial service among the poor gradually won over skeptics. They couldn't help falling in love with the light Teresa shone. India honored her work in 1963. In 1971, the Vatican awarded her with the Pope John XXIII Peace Prize. *Time* magazine called her a saint and put her on the cover in 1975. The rest of the world joined in celebrating Teresa's efforts in 1979 when she received the Nobel Peace Prize. Her acceptance speech offered an appropriate reflection of her ministry and her spirit.

> I am grateful to receive [the Nobel] in the name of the hungry, the naked, the homeless, of the crippled, of the blind, of the lepers, of all those people who feel unwanted, unloved, uncared-for throughout society, people that have become a burden to the society and are shunned by everyone.[12]

By that time in her life, Teresa was nearly seventy years old—her once-smooth skin wrinkled, her body bent, her attire aptly plain. Those who didn't know better might mistake her for Snow White's haggard witch. Unlike Diana, Teresa did not grace the cover of magazines because of her physical attractiveness. If anything, observers more endured than admired her appearance. Mother Teresa graced the cover of magazines because of a different kind of charm.

During the same week in 1997, the world mourned the loss of two women. Each had been on the cover of *Time*. Each was an icon to the world. Both were beautiful.

It has been said that beauty is in the eye of the beholder. On one level, I suppose that's true. From the first time I saw my bride-to-be, every other woman began to diminish. One who plays the piano can better appreciate a well-played concerto than the tone deaf. The amateur painter quickly sees the genius of a masterpiece, just as the baseball fan calls a perfectly executed double play beautiful. Our capacity to admire or perceive beauty varies according to individual passion or expertise.

But on another level, this isn't true. Certainly one "beholder" can appreciate different degrees and types of beauty more than another, but neither determines beauty itself. As Plato proposed, we see beauty in temporal things because of the existence of an ideal, transcendent beauty. Genuine beauty—that for which our hearts long—is not in the woman or the concerto or the masterpiece or the double play. Those things merely reflect it. Another philosopher, St. Thomas Aquinas, agreed:

> Thus, the beautiful is called that which participates in beauty; beauty is the participation of the first cause which makes all things beautiful. Indeed, the beauty of a creature is nothing but the likeness of divine beauty participated in things.[13]

In other words, God—the first cause—is ultimate beauty. He is, therefore, its standard and Creator. The things we admire around us but faintly reflect true beauty, like catching a whiff of a passing woman's perfume. We can like one perfume more than another, but they all share in common the characteristic of sweet, pleasant aroma. Nordstrom doesn't sell bottled stench.

We admired Princess Diana because she, perhaps more than most women, reflected the true form of physical beauty. The same can be said of countless other women, and to some degree, of them all. Whether seen in their eyes or their grace or their figure or their hair or their softness or their smile or their legs or in any number of characteristics, most women reflect a beauty that echoes true, pure femininity.

It also has been said that beauty is more than skin deep. Aquinas described one kind of beauty of the spirit and another of the body. We admired Mother Teresa because she, perhaps more than most women, reflected the true form of spiritual beauty. Whether seen in her kindness or her maternal nurturing or her selfless diligence or her love for discarded life or her quiet strength, Teresa was an icon of true, pure goodness. She provided a faint reflection of the kind of person we hope, or rather, we know God is.

If ultimate beauty were in the eye of the beholder, then beauty would be a matter of taste. If, on the other hand, beauty is in the eye of the Creator, then it becomes a matter of truth. When we appreciate beauty, we do not merely admire our own inclinations; we admire God's self-portrait. Here and there we catch a glimpse of his portrait. We long to see it in its entirety, a longing only briefly and inadequately satisfied by a pretty face, a stunning sunset, or a well-told story.

We've all met a person for the first time and said, "You look so familiar! Have we met before?" It is that way when we bump into beauty, whether physical or spiritual. Such encounters provide faint echoes of an ideal beauty we sense we've met before. They look so familiar.

We know that an engineer made our world because it fits together and runs so well. But our world is more than merely functional. It is also beautiful, made to be admired. And while we can appreciate bits of the beauty it reflects—a mountain range, blooming flowers, a running horse, a young woman's hair, an old woman's grace—its full beauty is known only to one. Ultimate beauty resides in those eyes alone. And only in that face can it be found.

INKLING
BEAUTY IS IN THE EYE OF THE CREATOR.

CHAPTER FIVE

Gulps of God

Our Father which art in heaven . . .
THE LORD'S PRAYER

Early morning on July 25, 1990, I
took my first sip of a drink that tastes like God. Life changed forever when our nine-pound, blood drenched, screaming baby Kyle
was born.

It happened again two, seven, and ten years later when Shaun,
Troy, and Nicole came along. Now I spend my days gulping the
good and the bad of what it means to be somebody's daddy, to be
their highest earthly representation of a heavenly person. I became
and am becoming something God has always been: a father.

While I don't do the job nearly so well, I can relate to how God
must feel as the One millions call "Our heavenly Father." My wife
shares the feeling, though in very different ways. If I represent God's
stability, provision, and strength, then Olivia shows his compassion, beauty, and tender caring. Together we give our children a
small taste of who he must be. We also share the moments that tell
us something of how he must feel, snapshots imbedded in the
heart's photo album.

Click—I recall the flutter of life as my hand rested on Olivia's
protruding belly, and the flutter of awe at the knowledge that

47

another human being, my child, would soon journey down the birth canal into a new world.

Click—I recall staring into each tiny infant face mere minutes, hours, and days after they'd been scrunched within the tiny space of mommy's womb. Miniature eyelashes, ears, and lips. Perfectly formed hands wrapped around my now giant index finger.

Click—I recall hour after hour coaching that first word until finally "dada" came out (sort of). No one else heard it, and it could just as easily have been any word in the dictionary. But it sounded close enough to give my life meaning.

Click—Cheering first steps into mommy's arms.

Click—Wiping first tumble-down-the-stairs tears.

Click, click, click—Accepting that first openmouthed, runny-nose-laced kiss, then wiping my face before getting two more.

Some of the most awe-inspiring moments come when I clearly see myself in one of the kids. Sometimes too clearly, like the time our oldest embarrassed his fifth-grade teacher by correcting her in front of the class. Totally inappropriate. Entirely out of line—but exactly the kind of thing I would have done at his age. Like his dad, he has a hard time letting an error go uncorrected. "You know, he takes after you in that way," my wife points out the painfully obvious.

I could do the same. Our second child reflects many of the strengths and weaknesses found in his mother. I see Olivia in Shaun just as clearly as she sees me in Kyle. Even more amazingly, we both see traces of ourselves in all of our kids. From the shape of a nose to the tone of a voice, each expresses our personhood in big and small ways. It is like an artist seeing a bit of himself in what he creates. The painting is wholly other, yet clearly from himself.

I think God allows us to become parents so that we can sample what it feels like for him to be our Father. He must feel about us the way I do my children. While wholly other, I am clearly from him. I can't help the love I feel for my children, like an irresistible impulse woven into the fabric of my being. So God must love his children. He can't help it.

At one and a half, Nicole has reached that phase when children get and give a kick out of identifying facial features. As with all children, she first mastered the nose. "Where's your nose?" I ask, eager for my budding genius to point to the center of her face. Then comes the really good part. She turns her finger around, points to my giant beak, and struggles to pronounce one of only twenty words in her developing vocabulary: "Nose." We then move on to other parts: eye, ear, cheek, hair. When we hit the chin, her tiny hand gently cups itself under my jawbone as my heart melts dead away. Her determined tenderness tells me the world and the people around her—the things we adults take for granted—are a marvel. Every new discovery becomes part of the adventure called learning. I love cultivating and watching the process. I love the sense of awe it reawakens in me.

I wonder: Does God's heart melt when I reach for his face, or when I struggle to put my discovery into words?

My older boys have reached that awkward stage between childhood and puberty when dad feels unsure whether to lovingly hug them good night or give them a fierce punch in the arm. They also are in that stage when I find myself amazed at who they are becoming. Shaun is the imaginative artist. His mind overflows with possibilities, reflecting them on the page. He hands me his latest creation, eager for my approval. "Good job, buddy!" An inadequate expression of how I really feel. He does with pencil and crayon what I do with words—making something out of nothing. The best ones end up in our collection of imperfect masterpieces.

Kyle is proving to be a gifted musician. I quit piano lessons long before reaching his current skill level on the keyboard. He has also done well with guitar and other instruments. As I try keeping the little ones quiet at Kyle's semiannual piano recitals, I can't believe my child has learned to play such difficult music. "That was great! I'm proud of you." Equally inadequate. But I really am.

I wonder: Does God's heart thrill when I mimic his ability to create something out of nothing? Does he get a lump in his throat when I use the talents he gave?

Of course, for every moment of parental pride, joy, or awe, there has been a moment of frustration, conflict, and heartache. They all come as a package. Our home has seen more than its share of irresponsible spills, nap-deprived tantrums, and willfully defiant rebellion. As the father, I routinely have to play the role of disciplinarian. I now hear my father's words coming out of my mouth.

"Don't speak to your mother like that!"

"Go to your room and wait for me."

"You have three seconds to change that attitude!"

I don't like being stern. But it is a necessary part of the job. I love my children too much to overlook wrong behavior. Still, it can be painful. No matter how many times I correct the kids, another round of conflict always looms on the horizon. You have to develop thick skin as the parent of young children. Being respectful doesn't come any more naturally for them than it did for you or me. It has to be learned. It has to be taught.

I wonder: Does our heavenly Father tire of our bad attitudes? Does he find it necessary to be stern at times, loving us too much to overlook wrong?

Every day I take another gulp of what God must feel. I can't help loving my kids, imperfections and all. I would die for them. I suppose he would too.

❧

When the disciples asked Jesus to teach them how to pray, he gave them a prototype. His words have become familiar to the religiously devout or to anyone forced to attend church as a child. Recall sixty-five of the most famous words Jesus ever spoke.

> Our Father which art in heaven, Hallowed be thy name. Thy kingdom come. Thy will be done in earth, as it is in heaven. Give us this day our daily bread. And forgive us our debts, as we forgive our debtors. And lead us not into temptation, but deliver us from evil: For thine is the kingdom, and the power, and the glory, forever. Amen.[14]

Millions of people recite those words every Sunday. But how many grasp the profound nature of the first two? Jesus invites us to call God "our Father." While only Christians believe Jesus is God, all major world religions claim to respect his teachings. And in this case, he taught us that God cares about the details of his children's lives. He concerns himself with our daily provision and with our right behavior. But then, what good father doesn't?

It is one thing to view God as a father. For some, the image brings wonderful memories of happy childhood days under the firm, loving protection of paternal care. For others, however, it can dredge up painful feelings of a dad who seemed always angry, self-consumed, or absent.

It is quite another thing to see God through the eyes of one who has been a father. I know what it is to see myself in my children and to derive my joy from their happiness. I know what it is to want to protect them from harm, yet realize that I must let them make and learn from their own mistakes. I know what it is to become angry at their disobedience while hating the need to punish. I know what it is to lay aside my own desires and dreams to meet the needs of my child.

In short, I know something of how God must feel, because he has allowed me a small taste of what it is to be somebody's daddy. And of the many things being a father has taught me about him, I am most certain of this one thing. God can't help loving us.

INKLING
GOD CAN'T HELP LOVING HIS CHILDREN.

PART II

THE PAIN
WE ENDURE

He jests at scars who never felt a wound.

WILLIAM SHAKESPEARE

CHAPTER SIX

Shadows

FAUSTUS: Tell me, then, thou Evil, who made thee?
MEPHISTOPHELES: He that made all things.

SCENE ONE OF *THE DEVIL TO PAY*

It is the day of my nephew's graduation ceremony with about twenty-five or thirty friends and relatives attending the drop-in reception. I am walking a cranky Nicole to the park and back, a much needed break for the baby and for me—and an opportunity to digest what I've experienced mingling with the crowd.

It is a happy event, an occasion to celebrate Nicholas's accomplishment and future. He will head off to Columbia University in the fall, the first in his family to go Ivy League. All feel glad for Nick, with lots of congratulating and well-wishing. Coordinated paper plates and punch cups and the obligatory bundle of helium-filled balloons tied to the back of one chair provide the perfect setting for uninteresting small talk and forced smiles. But below the surface of pleasant chatter and Nick's bright future, I sense dark shadows in the lives of one person after another.

Nick's mother, Terri, has a hard time focusing on the guests. Her older boy, Matthew, won't let her; he's demanding attention, as usual. Hard to blame him, since visiting his mother is a special treat these days. Matthew has lived in a group home for the handicapped since he became an adult, allowing Terri to have a life beyond the constant caregiving that defined his childhood years. I remember watching her in those days. She worked with Matthew so that he could learn to communicate despite near total blindness and hearing loss. Terri seemed the model of ruthless compassion— determined to help her son become the best his limitations would allow, in much the same way she insisted that the younger Nicholas become all that his exceptional gifts would allow. Today, the contrast between them is stark. If Nick shines the light of great potential, Matthew casts the shadow of severe limitation.

Carol is one of Nick's long-time neighbors. Very nice of her to drop by, especially in light of her recent struggles. She wears a lovely wig, covering what would otherwise announce her chemotherapy and radiation treatments. If you didn't know about her cancer, you wouldn't be able to tell. "I've just completed my second round of treatments." It is difficult to go through something so traumatic and have people unaware. "It seems to have been successful. I'm in remission." A hopeful sign, but the word "seems" keeps a chill in the air.

"That's wonderful news," comes the expected reply. "You look great!" Easy to say when you don't know what else to do. "Well, good to see you." Conversation over—not that Carol doesn't want to talk about it. It's just that others don't know how.

Another neighbor, Seth, also attends. Slightly older than Nick, his own graduation propelled him into the real world several years earlier. But the world that eagerly opens its arms to Nick has shown less of a welcome to Seth. You see, Seth has a severely deformed face. Several surgeries have helped—such as positioning hearing aids where ears are supposed to be—but they cannot cover like Carol's wig. Inadequate facial bone structure creates the appearance of one who has been either beaten, burned, or both. His appearance frightens my children. In truth, it probably frightens most adults. Shaun, ten years old, overreacts in embarrassing shock. "I hope I didn't hurt his feelings . . . ," he says in regret. I wonder whether countless others, caught by surprise over the years, share that regret. I suppose one in Seth's situation gets used to it. But then, maybe not.

Things take a positive turn with Roger and Teresa, newlyweds married less than six months. I've known Teresa for years, my wife's forever-single cousin. Suddenly, in her forties, she found Mr. Right. Roger seems very nice. A teacher and church worker, his quiet warmth seems impossible to dislike—unless you are his ex-wife. She left him for another man, abandoning a long-term marriage and two children for the promise of a better life. She probably didn't find it. But she nonetheless left the shadow of three broken hearts in the wake of her chase. Maybe Teresa can spark light into what must be some very dark hearts.

Teresa's sister, Jenell, seems glad she could attend. She spends much of her time caring for her once-strong father who now suffers the ravages of Alzheimer's disease. My wife, Olivia, does the same for her own mother. Both enjoy this brief reprieve from the ongoing heartache and frustration understood only by those who bear the burden of an aging parent's care.

And then there is Ron, Nick's justifiably proud father. What could feel better than watching your youngest son move the graduation cap tassel and point his shining star toward one of the nation's most prestigious universities? To top it off, Dan, his older boy from a previous marriage, seems to be doing well—working a good job, enjoying a lovely wife and kids. Despite Ron's smiling face, however, I wonder whether the joy of this day dims a bit at the memory of another—a day anything but happy. Years earlier, Dan's younger brother, Ron's second child, died from an illness medical attention might have prevented. But that son didn't care enough about life to bother. So death obliged. Whatever the reasons, whoever to blame, its tragic knife must have driven deep into Ron's heart. Can any father completely celebrate the achievements of one son without grieving the loss of another? I doubt it.

As I carry Nicole back inside and re-enter the party, gifts have begun to be opened and cake enjoyed. Laughter fills the scene, all focused on the bright graduate with an even brighter future. And yet, knowing the dark shadows in the lives of those around him, I foresee the possibility of his own. I hope Nick's life will be filled with nothing but light. Unfortunately, like everyone else in the room, I know better.

~&~

He was once the most famous American author in the world, the man who created such beloved characters as Tom Sawyer and Huck Finn. The world knew Samuel Clemens by the name of Mark Twain. His tales of life along the Mississippi met with phenomenal success, thanks to a quick wit and sharp intellect. The titles remain popular nearly a century after his passing, from *Huckleberry Finn* to *A Connecticut Yankee in King Arthur's Court*. But a book published after his death sheds important light onto the shadows of Mark Twain's soul.

His family feared the book would disparage an otherwise favorable legacy. Oh sure, Mark Twain had been irreverent; it was his trademark. But this book seemed different. Its sacrilege and cynicism revealed more of the man than his daughter, Clara Clemens, wanted known. And so it would not reach a wide audience until fifty years after Sam Clemens's death.

Mark Twain wrote *Letters from the Earth* during a difficult chapter in his life. While on a world speaking tour, a necessary evil for Clemens due to financial troubles, he received word that his beloved daughter had become deathly ill. Sadly, he could not return home before losing her, something for which he never forgave himself, or his God.

Many have described this incident as a turning point in Clemens's life. After that heartbreaking loss, he ceased to believe in a good God. A deity who allows such things was not, in his view, worthy of worship. And so, Mark Twain turned his creative gift into a weapon for spewing venom. The result was a collection of "letters" written by Lucifer to his fellow angels, describing the silly beliefs of religious humans.

Some of the material is quite funny, such as his description of the heaven we conceive—a place that has everything we dislike (harps) and nothing we like (sexual intercourse). But it quickly turns dark, such as his description of the commandments God has supposedly given.

> He says, naively, outspokenly, and without suggestion of embarrassment: "I the Lord thy God am a jealous God."
>
> You see, it is only another way of saying, "I the Lord thy God am a small God; a small God, and fretful about many things."
>
> He was giving a warning: he could not bear the thought of any other God getting some of the Sunday compliments of this comical little human race—he wanted all of them for himself.[15]

And one that seems directly linked to Twain's own loss. . .

> According to the belief of these people, it was God himself who said: "Thou shalt not kill." Then it is plain that he cannot keep his own commandments.[16]

Sam Clemens, when faced with life's pain, saw only darkness. His hope in the possibility of a good God died when his precious daughter took her last breath. He, like many, hit the wall of despair harder than expected. It happens all the time, prompting some of the most common and difficult questions in human experience.

"Why do bad things happen to good people?"

"How can a good God allow suffering?"

"Why is there evil in our world?"

All variations on the question posed by Shakespeare's great predecessor, poet and dramatist Christopher Marlowe. In his most famous play, *The Tragical History of Doctor Faustus*, Marlowe's central character, Dr. Faustus, confronts evil, personified in his antagonist, Mephistopheles. British playwright, Dorothy Sayers, powerfully captured his dilemma (and ours) in a contemporary retelling.

> FAUSTUS: Tell me, then, thou Evil, who made thee?
> MEPHISTOPHELES: He that made all things.
> FAUSTUS: What? Did God make thee? Was all the evil in the
> world made by God? Beware what thou sayest; I know thee
> for a false and lying spirit.[17]

Faustus, like most of us, jumps quickly to God's defense. He cannot accept the notion that God might not be good. Nor can we. Even as we shake an accusing fist at heaven over some disappointment, we secretly hope he isn't to blame.

But wishful thinking comes up short, and the question still haunts us. Philosophers and theologians have long debated the nature of evil. Is it real or an illusion? Is it an actual thing or merely the absence of something else? Did God make it, or did it come into being of its own accord? And if so, does that make God something less than omnipotent? After all, if he is all-good and all-powerful, shouldn't he have prevented evil's birth?

These questions get cast in an entirely new light, however, when Faustus poses the direct query we all yearn to ask.

> FAUSTUS: Answer again, and this time all the truth, art thou
> God's henchman or His master? Speak! Who made thee?
> MEPHISTOPHELES: God, as the light makes the shadow.
> FAUSTUS: Is God, then, evil?

MEPHISTOPHELES: God is only light, and in the heart of the light, no shadow standeth, nor can I dwell within the light of Heaven where God is all.[18]

Mephistopheles then explains that true light cannot create darkness—but anything that turns its back on light will see its own dark shadow.

I can see only two real options. Option one: A good God exists who allows his creation to turn its back on his light. Those who embrace this option see the shadow, driving them to seek the light. Option two: Evil rules the universe. Those who embrace this option see only darkness, and it drives them mad.

Blame the Devil, Adam's fall, or whatever scapegoat you wish. One thing is certain: you and I live with and see the shadow, something that can exist only in the presence of light.

INKLING

EVIL'S SHADOW ATTESTS TO GOD'S LIGHT.

CHAPTER SEVEN

Getting Back at God

Disbelieving in God was a good way
to get back at Him for the various things
which predictably went wrong in my life.

J. BUDZISEWSKI

As I entered the lecture hall lobby, an uptight man standing behind a folding table scattered with books and leaflets greeted me. At first, I mistook him for one of those religious fanatics who wave signs with misspelled words while barking at people. He certainly looked the part—a strange blend of quirky college professor and scruffy, homeless drunk. As it turned out, however, this man was no zealous believer. He was a zealous unbeliever, something that became apparent when I glanced at his selection of material.

He had about six books from Prometheus Press, a well-known atheist publishing house, and several small tracts, very much like the kind a street evangelist might distribute or a thick-headed Christian might give the waitress instead of a tip. But these tracts weren't created by believers to convert nonbelievers. They had been written from a nonbeliever to Christians. I thumbed through one of the leaflets, taking advantage of the idle moments before the event began.

Dear Christian: I have heard your message of salvation many times. . . . However, I am an unbeliever. It's not that I particularly

63

want to doubt; it's just that I have no choice. I have examined your claims and I am not convinced that they are true. I may even wish them to be true (or I may not)—but I am not so naïve to think that something can be true or false just because I desire it.[19]

The writer clearly viewed my faith as mere wishful thinking, like a child who invents a pretend playmate to avoid loneliness. I read on as the attacks moved from my intellect to whether my God is worth the effort.

> If the mind of a god is the measure for morality, then there is no way to measure if god's actions are "good." The murderous, sexist, intolerant activities of the biblical deity and the presence of chaos, ugliness, and pain in the universe portray your "supreme" god as supremely immoral, by my standards. I could invent a nicer god than that, and so could you.[20]

My atheist was starting to sound like one of those barking sign wavers. Still, he got me thinking—but only for a moment. My reading got interrupted when the moderator approached the microphone to begin the main event, a debate jointly hosted by the "Internet Infidels" and "Free Thinkers" at Colorado College. The topic: "Does God Exist?"

Both participants had a Ph.D. behind their names. Each taught philosophy at the university level. Each had examined the evidence—and come to dramatically different conclusions. One described himself as a theist; the other, an atheist. Actually, not a true atheist. By his own admission, it is impossible to prove a universal negative, such as the statement, "There is no God." So, rather than try to defend an indefensible position, he described himself as agnostic, one who believes we cannot know whether God exists.

For the next ninety minutes, each gentleman presented his case. The theist described how, while we may not be able to prove God's existence, the evidence for it is much stronger than the evidence against it, making it the more reasonable position. The agnostic, on the other hand, presented the reasons for his lack of belief, such as the problem of evil. After respectfully listening to one another, each challenged the other's points.

I found watching the audience of about two hundred more interesting than the debate itself. From their nonverbal reactions to the presentation, I discerned three distinct groups. First, I noticed those predisposed to reject God's existence, such as the book-table man I met in the lobby. I also observed those predisposed to believe in God, many of whom seemed to be members of the campus Christian club. Both groups responded positively to the debater with whom they agreed, disregarding or disparaging the other. But a third, smaller group seemed sincerely interested in both views. This handful of folks took notes, paused to reflect upon the statements made for and against, and mentally sorted through points and counterpoints—seemingly eager to grapple with life's most profound question.

After a brief break, the moderator moved into the final segment of the event, when the audience could ask questions.

Comments from the crowd confirmed my earlier impressions. The sincerely curious asked the best questions. The others displayed more demagoguery than inquiry, trying to convert the ignorant heathen or blaming believers for the Inquisition. Neither seemed very impressive, or effective.

Perhaps the most dramatic moment of the evening came when a woman approached the microphone, barely able to contain her anger. Thus far, questions had been posed in a respectful tone, even despite strong disagreement. Not this time. Probably in her early fifties, she looked much older, as if life had dealt her some very hard blows. She pointed an accusing finger and unloaded a lifetime of resentment upon God's defender.

"I want to know where this god of yours is when little children are abused or when people are buried under the rubble of buildings destroyed by wartime bombs!" Her face grew increasingly red as her volume increased. "I can't believe in a God that passively sits back and watches innocent people suffer." While her examples came from other sources, her passion betrayed a painful personal story. She moved from general objections to a personal attack. "You seem pretty healthy and happy to me. I don't sense you know what it is to suffer, to endure great loss and disappointment! From where you sit, it is easy to believe in a good God."

What she didn't know is that the man she accused of glibly presenting a good God without personal knowledge of pain was, in fact, suffering the greatest heartache of his life. His beloved wife, the mother of their two small children, had been enduring the uncertain ravages of chemotherapy—and he faced the very real possibility of losing her.

After several minutes of bitter accusation, the moderator interrupted the woman in order to provide opportunity for a response. The crowd grew hushed, some hoping the theist had finally met his match, others eager to hear how he would answer a question that they could not.

"I would like to ask you," came the surprisingly calm reply, "to whom you express this anger you feel? The God I know would welcome an opportunity to comfort you, as he does do many who suffer as you've described." Nice, but not really an answer. He continued. "You are right to feel a sense of outrage at the evil in our world. But your outrage poses a very important question. Upon what basis do you call one thing wrong and another right? Unless there is such a thing as good, we would not be able to recognize bad. So, your anger at evil points to the existence of the good—a perfect good that has its source in a perfect God."

Remarkable! He used the problem of evil as evidence for rather than against the reality of God. Yes, evil exists in our world. But without God, the ultimate standard of good, we have no basis upon which to condemn it. In short, every "Ought not be" points to the greater reality of an "Ought to be."

The anger of that woman and the book-table tract man suddenly made perfect sense. They both had recognized the second tenet of the human heart, that something is wrong. Expressing outrage at the cruelty of a broken world is perfectly appropriate. The problem is not in the anger, but in what we do with it. These people did not become atheists because they couldn't find evidence of a God. They became atheists because they wanted revenge.

Yale Ph.D. and University of Texas philosophy teacher J. Budziszewski can relate. He too was an angry atheist. He too pointed an accusing finger at those he considered mere wishful thinkers. In his words, "Because I believed things that filled me with dread, I thought I was smarter and braver than the people who didn't believe them. I thought I saw an emptiness at the heart of the universe that was hidden from their foolish eyes. Of course I was the fool."[21]

Today, he describes his folly as something motivated by anger. "Disbelieving in God was a good way to get back at Him for the various things which predictably went wrong in my life after I had lost hold of Him."[22]

Like many others, Budziszewski knew life as unfair. In suffering the bad, he lashed out against the possibility of the good. Of course, this created a problem. One can't cut the dead branch of evil from the tree of good while still seated on its limb. When we reject the good that God is, all that remains is the evil that he isn't.

"I knew that if there existed a horrible, there had to exist a wonderful of which the horrible was the absence. So my walls of self-deception collapsed all at once."[23]

Nineteenth-century poet and painter Rossetti once said that the worst moment for the atheist occurs when he feels really thankful and has nobody to thank. I believe the reverse is also true. When we grow angry at the pain of life, we need someone to whom we can express outrage—and seek comfort.

I encountered a profound inkling at that debate. I learned that our anger at bad suggests our desire for good, a good that can come only from God. When we reject his existence, we are like a hurt child screaming, "Get away from me!" at the parent eager to console. In truth, we fume at the pain—and we wish God would protect us from its reach and alleviate its touch. But that's something he can only do for those who believe that he exists and that he is good enough to care.

INKLING

OUR OUTRAGE AT EVIL POINTS TO A GOOD GOD.

CHAPTER EIGHT

Barney Theology

All you need is love.

JOHN LENNON

I have yet to meet a parent who likes Barney the Dinosaur. My own aversion began in 1992. Our first child had entered those wonderful toddler years when new words provide the daily family highlight—such as "bubble" or "ball" or, best of all, "daddy." Each day I looked forward to walking into the house to the sounds of my wife's "Daddy's home!" followed by Kyle's little feet running toward the door, arms outstretched for our ritual hug and tickle-fest. It was wonderful.

That is, until "he" entered the picture.

At about two years old, Kyle discovered Barney—which aired during the same thirty-minute slot as my homecoming. I will never forget the first time I walked in the door, heard "Daddy's home!" and waited for running feet that never came. Instead, Kyle's eyes remained glued to a hyperactive, purple lizard singing public domain tunes with altered lyrics. Go ahead, tear out my heart!

I have met very few kids who don't like Barney. It makes sense. After all, from a child's naïve perspective, what's not to like? Where else can you find a costumed grown-up who will dance and sing to you for thirty minutes, closing the experience with those affirming words, "I love you, you love me, we're a happy family." Sure, his voice sounds like a nerd with severe nasal congestion, but a very friendly nerd. And unlike Daddy, Barney never uses a stern voice, never says no, and never slaps your hand when you reach for the stove. Besides, Daddy will still be there to hug after the credits roll.

I often wonder whether we adults have our own version of Barney. He isn't a big, purple dinosaur, but someone we call God. He is not the real God, but the sort we prefer: a God always kind and who never says no or slaps our hand when we do something wrong. Our view of him has emerged out of what I call Barney Theology, a religious trend invading every faith tradition. Its one overarching conviction: God is love. Certainly, that is a good thing. I like love. I need love. But I need something more than love, as do we all.

I spent several years of my career reading letters sent to my radio-host psychologist boss. Many of the stories described actual childhood experiences worse than my most troubling nightmares. Folks wrote for advice, for comfort, or perhaps just because they needed to tell someone they didn't know personally. I remember one letter from a teen I'll call Alice, whose stepfather sexually abused her with the narrow end of a baseball bat. She described physical pain so intense it made her dizzy to the point of fainting. She described the confusion, wondering what she had done to deserve such abuse. She asked why God didn't stop it from continuing. I had read hundreds of letters describing sexual abuse, but this one boiled my blood like no other. I felt sick to my stomach, wishing I could get my hands on the man who would take a child's innocence in such a cruel, perverted manner.

I sometimes imagine what it must have been like for Alice growing up in such a home. I wonder what thoughts would run through her mind as she sat watching Barney the Dinosaur, listening to him sing his closing song. "I love you. You love me. We're a happy family." Would she feel affirmed with such a warm, verbal hug? Would she hear a message of happiness to help ease her pain? I doubt it. She would probably see right through its empty simplicity. She might laugh in scornful despair. Perhaps spit at the television screen. You see, that young girl knows that no song in the universe, regardless of how kind and affirming, can rescue her from the torture she endures—or the hate it inflames.

I wonder how Alice would feel sitting in a modern worship service, perhaps in one of those shopping-mall-sized evangelical congregations bustling with activity. You know the type—multiple services, coffee bar, bookstore, and a friendly yet efficient parking crew. Inside the service, thousands gather to participate in collective praise led by a cutting-edge band and large-screen projection. Everything is done with excellence, like well-produced television. Hands are raised. Faces smile. Tears flow. Beautiful melodies and energetic rhythms stir the soul. They celebrate a nice God, a God who loves everyone, forgives everything—more friend and lover than judge and jury.

But Alice doesn't relate. While certain of the reality of the experience of those around her, it doesn't connect to her own. The worship seems Pollyannaish—the songs of those glad for their happiness rather than desperate in their pain. Sure, it is nice to know God loves her in the midst of her abuse. But then, so does Barney.

Perhaps Alice leaves church and stops by her local bookstore. After grabbing a latte from the adjoining Starbucks, she takes a moment to scan the religious section. The title of a little book by Rabbi Harold Kushner grabs her attention, *When Bad Things Happen to Good People*. Kushner knows pain, not only because he ministers to many hurting people, but because his own precious son suffered and died from a rare disease that prevented proper growth and forced premature aging. Reading the tale of a little boy suffering while his helpless parents watch convinces Alice that

Kushner has honestly confronted a cruel world. He might have answers for her. He focuses on the book of Job, the story of a man who, like Kushner himself, suffered great loss and pain while his question "Why?" seemed to bounce off heaven's door. She flips to the conclusion to see what answers she might find.

> Are you capable of forgiving and loving God even when you have found out that He is not perfect, even when He has let you down and disappointed you by permitting bad luck and sickness and cruelty in His world, and permitting some of those things to happen to you? Can you learn to love and forgive Him despite His limitations, as Job does, and as you once learned to forgive and love your parents even though they were not as wise, as strong, or as perfect as you needed them to be?[24]

Kushner's God seems a kindly grandfather, cringing at the bad things happening to his beloved children. Forced to choose between an all-powerful God who allows suffering and an all-loving God with limited power, Kushner chooses the latter. His God seems feeble. He wants to stop our pain, but the bully of evil is younger and stronger. So God offers the only thing he can: consolation, sympathy, love. Nice, Alice reflects, but not enough.

Placing Kushner's book back on the shelf, Alice continues her search. She spots another best-seller, Neale Donald Walsch's *Conversations with God.* With millions of readers, she supposes, the author must offer something that can help her. Walsch says he has questioned God directly about life and recorded the responses. Maybe his more Eastern, pantheistic answers will provide what Alice needs. Thumbing through the book, she discovers a God even nicer than the one of Christians and Jews. He doesn't judge anyone for anything, and he asks Alice to go and do likewise.

> In the largest sense, all the "bad" things that happen are of your choosing. The mistake is not in choosing them, but in calling them bad.[25]

Evil is that which you call evil. Yet even that I love. . . . I do not love hot more than cold, high more than low, left more than right. It is all relative. It is all part of what is . . . I do not love "good" more than I love "bad." Hitler went to heaven. When you understand this, you will understand God.[26]

So, the problem is not what Alice suffers, but how Alice perceives the suffering. What she calls bad is part of what God loves. If Hitler went to heaven, then who is she to feel angry at her abuser? After all, God loves everyone. In the words of Barney, "We're a happy family."

None of these happy, friendly, nonjudgmental images of God can satisfy Alice. Her heart cries out for a God who gets angry, who hates evil, and does something about it. Alice wants—no, Alice deserves—more.

～☙～

John Lennon told us all we need is love. I disagree. Deep down, so do you.

On the surface, I like all of the ideals that fall under *love* in my religious glossary. Words like *kind, gentle, patient, nice, accepting,* and *nonjudgmental.*

On the surface, I do not like what falls in a different religious category. Words like *anger, wrath, law, condemnation,* and *hell.*

The former conjures images of Mother Teresa caring for the destitute and soup kitchen volunteers feeding homeless drunks. The latter suggests angry preachers shouting hellfire and brimstone.

But below the surface—on the level of reality that goes deeper than sentimental feelings—we know that if God is love only, he isn't enough. Barney theology turns the once grand contribution of religion into little more than a frail playground monitor pleading with earth's cruel bullies, "Please be nice." But what about when they don't heed our advice? What about when they aren't nice? Our emotions betray the God we thought we preferred.

If we get honest with ourselves, we don't want Hitler going to heaven. We want him to burn in hell for his crimes against humanity.

We don't want a child suffering because God can do nothing to stop it. We want to believe that even the bad can be used for some greater purpose, and that there will be eventual restoration.

We don't want Alice's abuser enjoying with impunity her perverse tortures. We want him to be judged and punished!

No matter how many Barney songs I sing about a God of love, my heart knows that the wrong in our world needs to be set right—something that will happen only when the one we want to see as nonjudgmental finally acts on his condemnation of evil and its perpetrators.

On one hand, I don't want to believe in hell. On the other, I hope with all my being that it exists. You see, I want a God who is more than love. I want a God who is justice, a God who sets things right, who punishes wrong and rewards right.

Like Alice, I want him to do it now. But I'll take it someday.

INKLING
If God is only love, he isn't enough.

CHAPTER NINE

Awkward Compassion

I'm afraid of that guy with the face.

FOUR-YEAR-OLD TROY

How was he?" asks Ryan's mother.

"Oh, we had a few problems. But he was great overall," I respond with a forced brightness. The truth is, Ryan was a nightmare, worst kid in the class that week.

"What kind of problems?" inquires Dad.

"Well, I spent a good portion of the hour chasing him all over the building because he didn't want to stay with the group." I can tell by the look on Dad's face that Ryan is going to be in trouble when they get home. Ryan can tell too. He starts apologizing like a drowning man screaming for a rope.

"That's all right, Ryan. We'll do better next time." I only half believe it, but it is the thing to say in such a moment.

"Why didn't you come get us out of the service?" asks Mom, the same woman who expressed relief when dropping off her son. She had said that she "really needed to go to church," clearly exhausted from a week of her own Ryan-chasing. Like several kids in this class, Ryan needs special attention. That's why we call it "Special Friends."

I almost had called them, fed up with her kid's inability to handle any sort of structure—and my own inability to figure out what might interest him. Our church has a number system that enables volunteers to summon a particular child's parent from the main worship service if problems arise. But I remembered Mom's exhausted face and couldn't bring myself to interrupt her one-hour break—her one hour of much needed refreshment.

"Listen, don't worry about it." She obviously felt concerned that her son might be wearing down every volunteer, causing them to abandon the special needs class or ban Ryan from attending. "You deal with his energy all week long. We can manage it for an hour. I didn't want to disturb you."

I don't know if what I said made her feel any better, but her thanks seemed sincere.

My wife and I periodically help out in various children's classes at church. Our rotation includes the special needs class. Usually only a handful of kids attend, with varying degrees of "special," including autism, mental retardation, physical disabilities, or like Ryan, severe Attention Deficit Hyperactivity Disorder. A handful in every sense of the word.

I find something uniquely rewarding about the Special Friends class. Sure, it can get chaotic, even frustrating. But something, well, special happens there.

I walk in confident, proud of myself for heroically filling the most difficult volunteer role, careful to mention which class I am teaching so that others can admire my servant heart. But by the time I walk out of the class, I feel completely inept. And completely in awe. Waving good-bye to the parents with a lump in my throat, the realization fills me that the true heroes are those worn down moms and dads who deal with such chaotic frustrations all week, all month, all year.

I become too easily annoyed with my kids when they forget homework or lazily neglect the passing ball during a soccer game. Ryan's parents would trade anything for such insignificant irritations.

Teenage Katie sits on the floor next to a toy while rocking herself back and forth the entire hour. Unlike us, her parents don't worry about how to pay for their daughter's college or wedding expenses. They worry about who will care for her when they become too old.

After church one Sunday I spoke to the Becks, parents of one particularly difficult special needs child. Their then six-year-old daughter, Maddie, had been born with a disorder so rare it had not been named. She required continual care and attention. They wondered aloud whether the church might start a program to help such families cope with the unrelenting stress. "It would mean so much to families like ours if we could just get a break now and again." Not that attempts hadn't been made. The typical, well-meaning volunteer came to the house to give the Becks a daylong break. Nervous about leaving Maddie with someone ill-prepared for her outbursts, aggression, and tantrums, they did their best to explain the task at hand.

"Don't worry about it," came the typical reply. "I'm sure we'll be fine."

Six to eight hours later, the Becks came home to an obviously frazzled volunteer who thinly veiled her relief at their arrival. "How was she?" they'd ask, bracing for the worst.

"Oh, she is such a precious little girl." True. "We had a fine time together!" A bold-faced lie. They knew their daughter had been her usual self and that the volunteer was trying to put a happy face on things. They also presumed they would never see her again. They were right.

I suggest they might prefer to hear something like "Your daughter was a pain in the rear. What time do you need me next week?" Their nods say it all. If only people would be real. Sincerely dishonest praise doesn't help. What helps is someone willing to help, despite the hard reality—something very few of us have the courage to do.

Most of us feel a bit awkward around those with special needs, at least until we build a relationship. I'm not sure why. It may have something to do with our desire to say or do the right thing without knowing what that right thing may be. Do we act as if nothing is wrong so the family feels as though they fit in? Or do we lower our voice and droop our eyes in sympathy for the heartache they endure? The former feels dishonest; the latter, condescending.

But our awkward feelings have a much deeper root. Such encounters confront us with the second tenet of the heart's creed. Our stomach becomes tense because the disabled know and quietly proclaim the undeniable reality that something is wrong. Seeing them trapped in a difficult experience reminds us that life is unfair. It raises questions with no easy answers. Why are some people healthy, beautiful, and driving red convertibles, while others spend a lifetime needing to be spoon-fed? Why is one child placed in the gifted track, another in special needs? Both sets of parents love their child and long to protect him or her from the hardships and heartaches of life. But the daily reality of the second quickly dispels any hope of success.

During a recent party I found my four-year-old son, Troy, hiding in the closet, frightened by a teenage boy with a deformed face (Seth, the boy you met in chapter 6). "I'm afraid of that guy with the face," he explained. So Olivia and I bring our boys with us when we volunteer in the Special Friends class. Partly for help, but mostly because we want them to push past natural kid fears of those who are different. We want them to become comfortable relating to the disabled.

I'll admit to subconsciously averting my eyes when walking past a person living with disability. I force them back to smile, greet, or do nothing, depending upon what seems appropriate. But the initial reaction still occurs, as if I am hardwired to avoid feeling awkward. It is like some internal mechanism of my heart tries to avoid tenet two, attempting to distract itself from what it knows true but wishes false. And so I, we, naturally turn away before willing ourselves back.

Not all force themselves back. I remember a conversation with a high-ranking official in then communist Russia. He was on a lecture tour in the United States and agreed to a question-and-answer session in our office. When asked his first impressions of our society, he made an interesting comment. "I am surprised by your compassion and care for the disabled." He then described our wheelchair ramps, special access restrooms, reserved parking, and other accommodations for the handicapped. "In Soviet Union, we do not have such things." Apparently, an atheistic society sees no particular reason to accommodate those unable to advance the collective good.

I also remember that Mother Teresa stuck out like a sore thumb in India precisely because she didn't accept the law of karma, a doctrine that serves as the foundation for ethics throughout the Hindu world (and other pantheistic faiths, called "New Age" in the West). Pantheism sees God as everything and everything as God. God is not a person we worship but a force in which we dwell. Its law of karma teaches that those who suffer are paying off debt from a former life, purifying themselves in this life so that they can reincarnate into something better, like a cow, in the next. The entire caste system depends upon the premise that we are destined to pay in one life for messing up in another. To help those suffering is to extend their payment plan. That is why the sick, poor, and disabled suffer so in and beyond India. Their suffering is meant to be. So, in the name of compassion, their religion tells them to avert their eyes.

Those who believe in a personal God, however, force their eyes back. They consider caring for the poor and disabled heroic rather than absurd. Survival of the fittest is a malady to cure, not a reality to accept. God cares for the needy through the heroic, through those willing to sacrifice themselves on behalf of another.

Our awkward compassion tells us something about God. It tells us why we turn our eyes away from pain, suffering, and disability. These things steal from the "something more" for which we were made. We don't like that. But it also calls us to lay aside selfish pursuits long enough to bring comfort, healing, and hope to those in need. It invites our participation in a process called redemption, replacing the "something wrong" we know with the "made right again" we want.

But redemption doesn't come easy. It requires a hero, like volunteers helping special need kids for an hour on Sunday. No—like exhausted parents loving their disabled child for a lifetime.

INKLING

GOD CARES FOR THE NEEDY THROUGH THE HEROIC.

CHAPTER TEN

The Square Peg

Nothing did so much to poison the last days of Ivan Ilyich's life
as this falseness in himself and in those around him.

LEO TOLSTOY

Her silence said everything. Already
we sensed that something must be wrong. That's why we made an
appointment.

During the fifth month, Olivia should feel the baby kicking,
should excitedly pull my hand onto her belly while lying in bed so
that I can feel it too. The baby seemed healthy weeks earlier—a
strong heartbeat prompting the usual excitement. When that
changed we became anxious, called the doctor, and obediently visited the radiology lab. The technician spread the gel and moved the
probe around my wife's abdomen, like she did during Kyle and
Shaun's stay in the womb. We saw faint images on the screen that
looked like a head and an arm, just like before. But this time was
different. I noticed the technician staring into the screen and making notes on the page, as if trying to avoid eye contact. She hates
this part of her job.

We drove to the doctor's office to learn the results. Only doc-
tors are allowed to deliver bad news. The trip remained quiet, both
of us feeling the dread of imminent grief. "I'm sorry about your
baby." The doctor's warm, compassionate voice opened the dike of
tears. As expected, our baby had died.

The next several hours were among the most traumatic of our lives—checking into the hospital, enduring five hours of induced labor, delivering a child who would never breathe. Since in the same hospital we had known the joy of Shaun's birth, the nurses sensitively put us in a room down the hall, away from the maternity ward. The last thing we needed to hear was the happy sound of crying newborns. The hospital reserved our hall for another kind of crying.

I managed to "remain strong" for Olivia until shortly after the baby's birth—or rather, death. Our friends arrived at the hospital with the older boys. Kyle was five, old enough to feel very excited about "baby Todd's" impending arrival but too young to understand the loss. I had the task of trying to explain to him something I didn't understand myself.

"The baby died," I said through a trembling voice.

Kyle's eyes immediately filled with tears. "Why?" came the question I couldn't answer. Just a few days earlier, Kyle had been making plans to play with his new sibling. Now, he was fumbling to fit the square peg of death into the round hole of life.

I suppose I could have said something about God taking Todd so that he could have another baby in heaven or that death is just a natural part of life. But I couldn't. Todd had simply died—it happens. And it is sad. So I explained that we had to love Mommy and cry together, which we did in the quiet hospital wing, now dark with sorrow.

I had encountered death before. Great Grandma Horan died when I was fairly young—but great grandmas are supposed to die. I lost Grandma and Grandpa Grey, and Grandma Bruner. Again, we expect death to take grandparents.

It took the death of Don, my best boyhood friend—killed at age twenty-one in a plane crash—to make death real to me. It stung. I watched a news report of a crash. Recognized the area as near my childhood home. Never expected to know anyone involved. Got a call hours later from a friend, saying Don was on that plane. Attended a memorial service without a body to view.

And then there was Cheryl, my thirty-something aunt, who was like a second mom. She knew the cancer would take her, so asked my wife and me to sing at her funeral. She loved a song titled, "Someday We'll Never Have to Say Good-bye." But we were saying good-bye. We wept more than we sang. Thirty-something is too young to die. So is twenty-one. So is the fifth month.

Fast forward five years. I bounce out the doors of that same hospital, this time joyously leaving the maternity ward. I head to my car in the parking lot, eager to pick up Kyle, Shaun, and three-year-old Troy, so that they can see Mommy and their new little sister. The ultrasound nurse had told us this was the girl we hoped for, but we had protected ourselves by only half believing it. "I'll believe it," I would joke, "when I don't see it!" It always got a laugh.

Skipping toward my car, I notice an acquaintance walking in the other direction, heading into the hospital. I remember his pregnant wife and flash a big smile. "We just had a girl!" I can't contain myself. "How about you?"

I spend the next few minutes listening. They had lost their baby, the little boy desperately wanted after having a girl. The pain in his voice reminds me of our own journey through grief over Todd. I say something inadequate about understanding what they are going through and get into my car. He gives a faint nod of appreciation and turns down the hall—away from maternity.

I sit quietly, reflecting before starting my engine. It seems strange but fitting that my round hole of new life would encounter death's square peg, forcing its way into another home. Sad for my friend but glad our grief had passed, I know that it will surely strike my home again. It might take a friend or a parent, my wife, or precious little girl. It will probably come unexpectedly, perhaps cruelly, but certainly unwelcome. And no matter how hard we try to "be strong" or try to accept death as "natural," we will cry.

⚬⚬⚬

A child gets struck down by a drunk driver. Another starves in a war-torn Third World nation, while a third is aborted before given a shot at life.

A woman suffers the cruel deterioration of Alzheimer's. Another passes peacefully in her sleep, while a third suffocates next to her daughter in a Nazi gas chamber.

A man hacks and coughs his lungs out from cancer caused by a lifetime of cigarettes. Another wastes away in a nursing home, while a third dies falling from a ladder in a freak accident.

No matter how it happens, death is never welcome.

It is a surprisingly short work. Usually we associate its author, Leo Tolstoy, with such classic tomes as *War and Peace* or *Anna Karenina*, volumes typically prominent on the shelf but too intimidating to actually read. This book is much easier, a story of about one hundred pages. Its brevity seems fitting, since it deals with a subject we don't like to talk about.

"The Death of Ivan Ilyich" has been hailed as one of the world's supreme works on the subject of death and dying. It tells the fictional tale of Ivan, an ambitious member of Russia's eighteenth century professional class. Relatively young, he has not given the inevitability of his dying a passing thought. But then a minor injury from a silly household accident unexpectedly triggers an illness that ultimately takes his life.

The reader travels with Ivan Ilyich through the valley of death's shadow, a journey filled with empty optimism and other forms of deception. It seems that everyone, with the exception of death's victim, wants to deny the reality his illness foreshadows.

> Ivan Ilyich suffered most of all from the lie, the lie which, for some reason, everyone accepted: that he was not dying but was simply ill, and that if he stayed calm and underwent treatment he could expect good results. Yet he knew that regardless of what was done, all he could expect was more agonizing suffering and death. . . . Nothing did so much to poison the last days of Ivan Ilyich's life as this falseness in himself and those around him.[27]

The lie produced an unwillingness, or inability, for anyone to offer the kind of compassion Ivan craved. They pretended, allowing them to avoid facing the horror Ivan could not, leaving him alone in his dread.

We quickly judge Ivan's friends and family, but their characters simply reflect our common reaction to death. We too avoid its terror by pretending—avoid its truth with lies. We replace tearful silence with well-intentioned but idiotic pep talks. Humble resignation gets drowned out by defiance, denial, or blame.

Finally, in a last-ditch effort to fend off terror, we concoct the final lie. "Even if death comes, it is nothing to fear. Like childbirth, it is a natural part of life's cycle." Of course, deep down, we know better. If birth is a leaping dolphin, death is a circling shark.

I believe that grief and fear are proper responses precisely because death is unnatural. God is the source of life. So life reflects his nature—natural. Death doesn't—unnatural. Certainly, everyone dies. But the fact that something bad happens to everyone doesn't make it good. The heart's creed says something is wrong, not everything is right. And we never become more aware of what's wrong than when we grieve a loved one's death—or fear our own. Like a hand reacts to the match's flame, our lives rightfully flinch at death's assault.

Entering the nursing home to pick up Grandma Olive, we walk down a hall one would avoid if possible. Most of the residents look in the final stages of life—or the early stages of death. Only the electronic glow and competing sounds of sitcoms, game shows, and weather reports infuse any illusion of activity. Based upon some reactions to our noisy children, the sound of young life seems unwelcome in this wing, much like the one down from the maternity ward. The last thing those in death's waiting room want to hear is crying children. Their hall is reserved for another kind of crying: the chronic, lonely sorrow of a lie that steals the compassion they deserve. Friends and family ignore most of them. I guess dolphins flee when sharks circle. Those who do visit shout silly pep talks about "looking good" and "the fun of craft class," as if nothing serious is wrong.

But something is wrong. It is something we fear and something we grieve. As well we should.

INKLING
WE GRIEVE DEATH BECAUSE GOD IS LIFE.

PART III

THE WONDERS
WE CREATE

For we put the thought of all
we love into all that we make.

J. R. R. TOLKIEN

CHAPTER ELEVEN

Seeing It

The evidence is not yet in.

CARL SAGAN

It had remained on the *New York Times* best-seller list for months. Smart people all over the world bought it. A few of them even read it. The author, theoretical physicist Stephen Hawking, graced the cover, his distorted frame not quite filling his crumpled suit or the specially equipped wheelchair that meant freedom from a life of immobile silence. Trapped inside a severely handicapped body, unable to talk without a computer-aided speech program, nonetheless he ranked as one of the great minds of the twentieth century. The Albert Einstein of our generation, he held Sir Isaac Newton's chair as Professor of Mathematics at Cambridge University.

My 1989 reading group chose his book *A Brief History of Time* as our monthly selection—partly because it interested us, but mostly because we wanted to be seen carrying it around. (Truth be told, I usually moved the bookmark further in than I had actually read to impress those who might notice.) I did manage to finish the book, which is more than can be said for most of my fellow showoffs. As a result, our discussion focused primarily on the first fifty pages. The book, like its author's mind, intimidated most of us. We tried to engage Hawking's thesis, even argued some of his points. But we did so hesitantly, recognizing how far out of our league he was. And so, after an hour of talk, only one thing became clear: our next selection would be simple fiction.

What happened to me reading Stephen Hawking mimics in some ways what has occurred in the Western world over the past few centuries. Once upon a time, we learned from prophets, philosophers, and priests. But the Enlightenment brought us a new authority: the scientist. Through rational observation of the physical world, science promised to reveal truth. We now all but worship the brilliant scientist who seems able to decipher this universe we inhabit, bowing in deference to those who answer profound questions we never thought to ask. Clearly smarter than ourselves, we accept their explanations—or at least, silence our doubts to avoid sounding dim-witted. And so we carry their books, if for no other reason than to look clever.

Who could blame us? Knowledge has increased at a dramatic pace, bringing such marvels as antibiotics, Apollo 11, and Nintendo Game Cube—miracles confirming our new faith. We began to see every human being living before the Enlightenment as, well, unenlightened. We even labeled their era "the Dark Ages." Mankind watched in self-satisfied amazement as Neil Armstrong took our one giant leap. We thump our proud chests because we can point to a black hole and offer mathematical theories for how it might work. Our kids spend countless hours enamored by computer-generated replicas of a real world they scarcely notice. It seems to me, however, that such accomplishments should drive humility, not arrogance. We are children exploring, not gods creating.

I don't know whether Stephen Hawking believes in God. Occasional comments suggest the possibility. "It would be very difficult to explain why the universe should have begun in just this way," he says at one point, "except as an act of a God who intended to create beings like us." It is refreshing that, despite his superior intellect, Hawking remains humble enough to acknowledge that some questions fall outside the expertise of scientific observation. "Up to now," he reflects,

> most scientists have been too occupied with the development of new theories that describe what the universe is to ask the question why. On the other hand, the people whose business it is to ask why, the philosophers, have not been able to keep up with the advance of scientific theories. In the eighteenth century, philosophers considered the whole of human knowledge, including science, to be their field and discussed questions such as: Did the universe have a beginning? However, in the nineteenth and twentieth centuries, science became too technical and mathematical for the philosophers. Or anyone else except a few specialists. . . . What a comedown from the great tradition of philosophy from Aristotle to Kant![28]

Bingo! Rather than using science to confirm the explanations of religion and philosophy, we used it to replace them, eventually relegating both to the back of the intellectual bus. Our impressive explanations of what and how made us lose track of why and who. We cut ourselves loose from the tether of humility.

Shortly before his death in 1996, Carl Sagan received a letter. As a world-renowned astronomer and media darling of the intellectual elite, Sagan had grown used to being inundated with mail. My friend and colleague, Bob Garner, wrote this particular note. Long impressed and intimidated by the mind of Sagan, Bob could not comprehend how such apparent brilliance could reject God's existence after a lifetime examining the order of our universe. How could Sagan, in the opening of his famous Cosmos series, say with a straight face, "The cosmos is all that is, or ever was, or ever will be"?

Bob did not expect a reply but received one nonetheless: Sagan's standard form letter, sent in response to Cosmos praise mail. At the bottom, however, appeared a brief postscript.

> What you suggest about religion is certainly possible.
> The evidence is not yet in.

I never met Carl Sagan and have no desire to judge his motives. If it's true that we face God in the afterlife, he doesn't need me to add to his present troubles. I'd like to think of him as a nice man sincere in his atheism. After all, why would anyone want to believe we live in a world without design or purpose?

Yet I share Bob's perplexed reaction to Sagan's note. After a lifetime staring at the evidence, he claimed it was "not yet in." Why couldn't he see it? Did he simply miss it, like a blind spot in the rearview mirror? Or did he ignore it, like closing one's eyes to an oncoming train? Did he observe the evidence and draw an honest conclusion against God? Or was he like Francis Crick, the Nobel Laureate who, after observing the mind-boggling complexity of DNA, warned, "Biologists must constantly keep in mind that what they see was not designed, but evolved."[29] Are these scientists truly unconvinced, or just stubbornly unmoved? I don't know.

I do know that at times I feel intellectually bullied, half accepting the accusation that I see God's hand because I need to see it, like a child needs to believe in Santa because he wants presents.

Call me simple if you like, but I prefer accepting the obvious. You can admire a masterpiece only so long before questioning those who deny its artist. You need only use a computer to realize someone programmed its software. As philosophy professor Peter Kreeft put it, "Some truths are so obvious, only the experts can deny them."

Astronomer Hugh Ross calls the cosmos the fingerprint of God.[30] Observing the same masterpiece, he draws a conclusion vastly different from that of Carl Sagan. Is he imposing religious belief onto scientific observation? Or has Ross, unlike many of his colleagues, simply retained the tether of humility, enabling him to see the obvious?

As we explore the wonders of human discovery and innovation, we need that same tether. Be it scientific discovery, artistic expression, or medical breakthrough, human invention is nothing more than entering into a creative process launched long before any of us appeared on stage. It is what J. R. R. Tolkien called "subcreation," using what *is* to develop what *can be*. The basic stuff of innovation has been placed before us, a fully equipped workshop awaiting its craftsman. Computer programmers gave Stephen Hawking the ability to speak. Divine creativity made the brain that gave him something to say.

I am proud of my fellow human beings for harnessing the power of gravity to reach the moon. But I am humbled knowing that same gravity was designed to keep me from flying off the earth.

I am impressed viewing Michelangelo's sculpture of David. But I stare in silent awe before the transcendent beauty it can only mimic.

I am glad that medicine offers vaccinations and penicillin to improve my health. But I feel grateful to God for the immune system that both merely assist.

I love my microwave oven, laptop computer, and front-wheel-drive minivan. I would hate to return to the "good old days" when a simple infection might kill my precious little baby because we had no pink medicine. I like talking on the phone to my wife while on a business trip and sending an email to those I'd rather not talk to. Let's face it, man has accomplished some terrific things. But it is God who gave us the inclination and capacity to do so. Advances in science and innovative ideas merely announce an ever-increasing human ability to observe, decode, and synthesize what already exists. Our "greatness" is based upon an ability to notice and admire, imitate and enhance.

Socrates had the right idea. Surrounded by modestly smart people who thought themselves brilliant, he enjoyed asking tough questions that revealed their ignorance or inconsistency. He did it so often, in fact, that the elite of his day considered him a nuisance. Eventually, they placed him on trial and required an explanation of his game. Plato records his defense in one of his most famous dialogues, *The Apology*.

Socrates defended himself by explaining that he did not intend to embarrass anyone or undermine common beliefs but rather to learn from those who seemed to have wisdom. The problem was, he found few good answers. As might be expected, this made people angry because, in his words, "my hearers always imagine that I myself possess the wisdom which I find wanting in others: but the truth is, O men of Athens, that God only is wise; and by his answer he intends to show that the wisdom of men is worth little or nothing."[31]

In some ways, Socrates was like my four-year-old son asking a simple but profound question, the kind I should be able to answer but can't. When I stammer and bluff in embarrassment, it lets air out of the illusion of adult omniscience. Troy doesn't claim to know the answer. He just wonders why I pretend I do.

After observing such pretense (or worse, self-delusion), Socrates comes to this conclusion:

> Well, although I do not suppose that either of us knows anything really beautiful and good, I am better off than he is, for he knows nothing, and thinks that he knows; I neither know nor think that I know. In this latter particular, then, I seem to have slightly the advantage of him.[32]

Socrates, like a questioning child, was humble enough to see it.

Carl Sagan, like the embarrassed adult, wasn't.

INKLING

GOD'S CLUES OF HIMSELF ARE OBVIOUS TO HUMBLE EYES.

CHAPTER TWELVE

Tunes of God

I will sit and hearken, and be glad that through
you great beauty has been wakened into song.

J. R. R. TOLKIEN, FROM *THE SILMARILLION*

I am one of millions walking the
earth who can be heard from time to time saying, "I wish I had
stuck with piano lessons." Feelings of shameful regret among us
quitters usually get triggered by the finger magic of one who
didn't—someone with the self-discipline as a child to remain
indoors on sunny days, refuse neighborhood pick-up games, and
practice boring scales while the rest of us watched *Gilligan's Island*.
Truth be known, we now greatly admire and secretly hate those
kids. Showoffs! Every perfectly performed triplet feels like a knife
in our hearts. They might just as well stick out their tongues in a
manner that says, "I'm a far better human being than you undisci-
plined losers!"

Not that there is any need for further humiliation. We remain
all too aware of our failure and the intense disappointment we are
to parents who invested thousands of hard-earned dollars into our
budding music careers. My shame exceeds that of most because
God directly helped to orchestrate my opportunity.

I was about ten when my parents prayed for a piano. Already
trying to feed seven children, they couldn't afford to buy one. Yet

they wanted to give my older sister and me a chance to take lessons. Of course, none of us expected such a big request to be answered. Our family rarely asked God for anything bigger than our daily breadbox. So imagine our surprise when, after only a few months, God pulled it off. A church acquaintance of my grandmother was replacing his old baby grand, which somehow made its way to our living room. It dwarfed the allocated space and Mom would have preferred a petite upright that fit more decoratively into the corner. But who argues with God when he gives such a nice gift? And so, at that tender age when boys show more interest in baseball and banana seat bikes, I began my journey into the challenging world of piano lessons.

To my credit, I lasted over three years—long enough to approach the level where folks enjoy more than tolerate your play. My parents did everything they could to keep me motivated. I remember one birthday when they bought me a four-album set of piano concertos by Wolfgang Amadeus Mozart. I had become interested in Mozart during music appreciation class at school. His story of composing at the age of four inspired my own attempts at the age of twelve. I even began writing some of my own simple pieces, one of which got fifteen minutes of fame. My piano teacher, our church organist, kindly added a few missing ingredients to my best composition and played it during a Sunday morning service. I felt so proud as I left the church service that day, hearing my simple tune bellow forth in such grand form.

Still, it wasn't enough. On the verge of greatness, nearly good enough to advance into book seven of the Schaum series, my drive got dashed on the rocks of boyhood interests. So I walked away from what could have led to fame, fortune, and Carnegie Hall. Disgraceful!

But I don't count it all loss. Piano lessons may not have made me into a child prodigy like Mozart, but they did plant a love for music that has since blossomed. When your fingers have tangled attempting Bach's *Inventions,* you have greater capacity to admire its proper performance. One who has composed a basic Sunday morning organ tune can better recognize the brilliance of a John Williams score or the striking simplicity of a John Lennon tune.

For me, music has become far more than mere background listening. It is how I hear beauty in a world filled with ugliness, the means through which a man can express the very soul of God. It is a gift to and from those disciplined enough to master its scales and discern its patterns. Music allows us to share what the heart feels, to touch the transcendence it knows to be real. Something I recognize when I hear it and that I long to enter.

I sure wish I had stuck with piano lessons.

God gave us just seven notes, plus sharps and flats, the basic building blocks with which we have written an infinite variety of music. Every tune expresses or triggers a vast array of human emotions. My preprogrammed radio buttons and CD collection give a small sample of that diversity. I choose one over another depending upon my mood.

Driving to work, top forty hits invite much needed adrenaline.

Driving home, country ballads help me wind down and perhaps drown my sorrows.

When writing, I prefer the inspiration of a movie score.

When reading, the quiet contemplation of a string symphony or gentle jazz.

The kiddie car pool means high-energy fun with contemporary bands.

Friday date night requires a romantic love song while holding my wife's hand.

And after dinner cleanup demands Celtic tunes so toddler Nicole can keep me entertained by dancing an awkward jig.

I don't relate to those who enjoy only one type of music. Depending upon the time, place, and setting, I love most styles, some of which have been my friends for decades. I've added others as I've aged. And the more diverse my taste becomes, the more amazed I feel at what music, in all its forms, says of God.

God did not write every song. He instead gave a basic scale and left the composing to us. Yet, on another level, every note seems part of a grand symphony that envelops all others. Like my own simple tune that became something greater when my teacher added missing ingredients, so God lets us participate in his performance. The melodies we create seem small, imperfect movements of something more. Our best performances awaken rather than satisfy the desire for a true music that we long to hear.

J. R. R. Tolkien created a fantasy world known as Middle Earth, complete with its own creation myth. In the opening of *The Silmarillion,* Tolkien tells the story behind the story. Long before the days when Hobbits and Ents sang simple songs of lore, much greater beings performed. It began with Iluvatar, creator of all things, and his angelic servants, called Ainur.

> And it came to pass that Iluvatar called together all the Ainur and declared to them a mighty theme, unfolding to them things greater and more wonderful than he had yet revealed; and the glory of its beginning and the splendour of its end amazed the Ainur, so that they bowed before Iluvatar and were silent.
>
> Then Iluvatar said to them: "Of the theme that I have declared to you, I will now that ye make in harmony together a Great Music. And since I have kindled you with the Flame Imperishable, ye shall show forth your powers in adorning this theme, each with his own thoughts and devices, if he will. But I will sit and hearken, and be glad that through you great beauty has been awakened into song."[33]

Tolkien's imaginary world, like our real world, was not just created—it was composed. Iluvatar, like the God he represents, is a great musician who has written a theme that he invites us to "adorn, each with his own thoughts and devices." Whether that adornment takes the form of an awe-inspiring Mozart concerto, a playful Beach Boys beat, or an ominous film score, it awakens great beauty into song.

Sometimes, the beauty is tragic, like the sorrow of death. Why? According to Tolkien, a dissonant melody has entered the world. In his myth, the introduction came through rebellion.

> But as the theme progressed, it came into the heart of Melkor to interweave matters of his own imagining that were not in accord with the theme of Iluvatar; for he sought therein to increase the power and glory of the part assigned to himself.[34]

And once introduced, the sour notes began to spread.

> Some of these thoughts he now wove into his music, and straightway discord arose about him, and many that sang nigh him grew despondent, and their thought was disturbed and their music faltered; but some began to attune their music to his rather than to the thought which they had at first.[35]

Anyone familiar with the Christian concept of Satan, also known as Lucifer or the Devil, will immediately recognize its influence upon Tolkien's mythology. But even those who subscribe to another or no religious perspective will resonate with the reality he portrayed.

We all know the tension of an unresolved chord and the slow torture of a voice off pitch. We expect music to convey beauty, even when tragic. We can't bear it any other way. When music is wrong, it must be made right—or it will drive us mad, because we were made for the something more that discord mocks.

And so, I am grateful to those of you who practice your instruments and rehearse your voice. Thank you for taking the seven basic notes of the scale and expressing what my heart both feels and longs to know. I appreciate the smile you bring to my baby girl's face while dancing her jig, and the tear in my wife's eye while watching a sad movie, and the rest you give my weary soul at the day's end, and the unspeakable thrill I feel as the music swells into what must be the voice of redemption—telling me that no matter how tense today's melody may seem, all will someday be resolved.

Thank you all for reminding me that God is life's composer—and our songs a small sample of the amazing symphony he wants us to hear.

Whatever you do, please don't quit.

INKLING

GOD IS THE ORIGINAL COMPOSER.

CHAPTER THIRTEEN

From Cave to Gallery Walls

Art is the signature of man.

G. K. CHESTERTON

My son Troy recently mastered the art of coloring inside the lines. Four years old and all boy, that is no small accomplishment. It takes great concentration, often requiring such ancillary measures as positioning his face a few inches above the picture and squeezing his tongue tightly between his lips. Not that long ago, the result looked less than impressive—Crayola spasms all over the page with little reverence for the intended picture.

"Wow, this is terrific!" I lied when presented with his messy attempts. A few moments later you could find that same picture buried under a cereal box in the laundry room trash container. But Troy kept working, and some of his more recent masterpieces have made it onto the refrigerator door, our most prestigious gallery of artistic expression.

A few years ago I visited the National Art Gallery in London, an enormous building filled with original works from centuries past, including paintings by Rembrandt, daVinci, Monet, and van Gogh. My tour of the gallery vacillated between moments of inexplicable awe and times when I wondered, *What were they thinking?* Many paintings provoked a tremendous sense of inspiration, spiritual sensations that drew me closer to transcendent realities often captured in great art. In this category I include Rembrandt van Ryn's portrayal of the woman taken in adultery, drawing the eye to a dimly lit scene of forgiveness and hope amid a dark, shadowy backdrop. There was also *Le Chateau de Steen,* by Peter Paul Rubens, a single gaze drawing one into the reality that the imperfect beauty we experience in this world is but a hint of real beauty yet to be known.

Other paintings, from my perspective, seemed far less impressive. Of course, I didn't say anything at the time. It would have been inappropriate, if not embarrassing. Glancing out the corner of each eye, it became apparent that those to my right and left saw something I somehow missed. Like most people, I had taken an art appreciation class in high school where instructors educate you to admire what doesn't immediately strike you as brilliant. Still, I could not remember what it was I was supposed to appreciate about Joseph Mallord William Turner's *Snow Storm,* or *Combing the Hair* by Edgar Degas. I could only wonder why these and other artists made the gallery despite what appeared to be coloring outside the lines.

Certainly, my reactions to such highly regarded art said more about me than the artists. After all, I am one of those who buys art based upon whether it matches the furniture. Despite my amateurish appreciation, however, I know that art is the signature of man. Whether that signature is a masterpiece worthy of the refrigerator gallery or a mess we must force ourselves to admire, man's artistic expression reveals something vital about who we are and who God is. To understand why, we visit the world's childhood by peering at cave walls.

In response to popular mythology about ancient man, G. K. Chesterton challenged what he considered unfounded assumptions, like the idea that our ancestors amounted to little more than upright brutes, or that males bonked females on the head before dragging them home to wedded bliss. "When novelists and educationists and psychologists of all sorts talk about the cave-man," wrote Chesterton, "they never conceive him in connection with anything that is really in the cave." He wondered, why not look at the only hard evidence we have by asking one simple question: "What did the cave-man actually do in the cave?"[36]

When we strip away our preconceived notions about the life of the caveman and look at his walls, we discover that early man— like modern man—was an artist. He drew and painted, mostly deer, horses, and other animals. On the whole, his walls look like a child's nursery—only instead of Mickey or Pooh, we see Bambi. Who knows? Maybe children were the artists, the cave wall serving the same purpose as my refrigerator door. The only thing we know for sure about ancient man is that, as Chesterton put it, "This creature was truly different from all other creatures; because he was a creator as well as a creature."[37]

Whatever else he is, man is an artist. He always has been and always will be an artist. Our creativity reflects and declares our Creator.

~∞~

When I look at a masterpiece that man creates, I see something of the masterpiece that he is. When I look at what he creates, I see hints of that for which he was created. Art provides evidence that we were made for more.

Whatever its form—sculpting, drawing, painting, still photography, film production—art plays a vital part in our inklings of God.

First, art reaches. More precisely, it shows us reaching for something. When Michelangelo began chiseling a large block, he did not chip away random chunks of granite, hoping something of beauty might show up. He reached for something specific, hidden deep within the stone—eventually releasing some masterpiece such as *David* that already had taken form in his imagination. When Charles Schultz sharpened a pencil and began to draw, he did not merely doodle to see what might happen. He reached for a smile that could transcend life's frustrations by creating a cartoon character named Charlie Brown. When Peter Paul Rubens began swiping his brush across canvas, he sought to portray some specific image, whether the sacred scene of Christ's descent from the cross or the sensuous myth of the feast of Venus.

Artists express our collective yearning for that which we were made to know and that which we are trying to recapture. They are reaching. They reach for a beauty we've never seen but know exists, a beauty that God is and that we were meant to reflect. But not all artists depict beauty. Much art portrays a dark, invading ugliness— what we experience rather than what we desire. Others shine a flickering light, the hope of eventual joy invading the shadows of pain. Regardless of the specific expression, however, all art has a common object: the heart's unspoken creed. Art declares that we are made for more, that we know something is wrong, and that we long to recover the lost beauty of life. It reaches for all three.

All art reveals something about the artist. Have you ever noticed how often a work of art directly or indirectly reflects the artist's religious (or antireligious) sentiment? From the famous portrayal of God's extended finger creating Adam on the Sistine Chapel ceiling, to the controversial painting of a cross submerged in human urine, art reveals something of the artist. Our beliefs, attitudes, struggles, and questions all spill forth onto the page, canvas, or screen. So does the philosophy of our times.

Francis Schaeffer, a spiritual and intellectual giant of the twentieth century, showed me how what an artist believes dictates what he creates. In his famous book *The God Who Is There*, Schaeffer walks us through the progression of Western philosophy and culture, showing how what professors taught found its way into what artists painted. Sadly, in the modern era philosophers declared God dead. As a result, the all-encompassing cohesion he brought to every other aspect of culture died too. We crossed a line of despair, sucking the light of hope from our creative expression.

Case in point, Vincent van Gogh. Taking seriously the necessary despair of a world without God, he painted a world without unity—and then took his own life. Tragic? Yes. Shocking? Not really. After all, life without God is meaningless, and suicide, an honest response. He took his professors seriously, and it drove him mad. As Schaeffer put it, "The death of hope in man had taken place in van Gogh. He died in despair."[38]

When art ceases to reflect what should be, all that remains is to express what is. It fixes our eyes upon valley shadows rather than the surrounding mountain peaks (and what may lie beyond). As a result, our big picture becomes a very small scene. Certainly, something is wrong with the world in which we live, and art should reflect this second tenet of our unspoken creed. But its ultimate purpose is much higher. Art can lift our eyes, reminding us of a reality for which we are made and seek to recover. It does this best when the artist heeds all three suspicions of his or her heart.

Art does one more thing. Picture the scene: an art enthusiast named Victoria on a date with an art imbecile named Biff. They are visiting a museum because she took his "Where would you like to go?" at face value. (Victoria doesn't realize that Biff hoped she liked professional wrestling matches and monster truck rallies.) And so, they stroll hand-in-hand through the gallery—she eagerly describing favorite artists, he silently pondering his predicament. But then, at a most unexpected moment, just when Biff had lost all hope of a second date, both sets of eyes come to rest on the same painting, perhaps *Olympia* by Edouard Manet. Victoria admires it because she knows the artist considered it his greatest work. Biff admires it because Olympia is nude. Despite the vastly different motivation of each, they share a common response: both hearts roused by the way the painting touches a deeper beauty each desires. They look, they discuss, they head off to Starbucks and fall madly in love. That's *amore!*

Art inexplicably triggers a reaction within every onlooker, the passionate and the passive alike. Yes, it reaches. Yes, it reveals something about its creator. But it also stirs something within me. Something I can't explain. Something I desire or fear or hate or love. It draws me out of myself and into another dimension. In the words of nineteenth-century writer George MacDonald: "Some dreams, some poems, some musical phrases, some pictures, wake feelings such as one never had before, new in colour and form—spiritual sensations, as it were, hitherto unproved."[39] In short, art tells me something about myself. Something I may have forgotten but always hoped true. I am the creation of a brilliant artist.

INKLING

OUR ART SPEAKS OF OUR ARTIST.

CHAPTER FOURTEEN

The Lego Box

The more enlightened we are the more greatness
and vileness we discover in man.

BLAISE PASCAL

I estimate that our house contains
approximately 10,000 Lego pieces. Not the big blocks like I used as
a boy, but the tiny, new generation Legos. Most of the individual
pieces remain sorted by color and size in a large, four-drawer plas-
tic container purchased after we gave up the impossible task of
keeping each kit in its original box. The rest are randomly and inexplicably scattered throughout every other room in the house, often
discovered while walking barefoot in the dark. The scream of pain
is actually good news because it means someone found what might
be an essential piece for Shaun's next creation.

All three of our boys love Legos. But our second, Shaun, is the
biggest fan. Like most kids, when we buy him a new kit, he immediately assembles the pattern on the box. But that pattern will never
show its face again. The pieces will become components for his
own original creations, most of them quite impressive works of
childhood engineering. And so it did not come as a big surprise
when, at nine years old, Shaun announced his career ambition: to
become a Lego engineer. I first reacted by mumbling a casual,
"That's nice," the way I had when he said he wanted to be a Jedi

knight. But then I realized just how cool and realistic the idea might be. After all, someone has to design the endless variation of kits that go onto store shelves and end up in our four-drawer container. From simple trucks to elaborate, mechanically enabled super systems, an engineer stands behind every new Lego model. Why not my son?

Shaun always has been into inventing. The latest and greatest technology fascinates him, and he remains firmly convinced he is the guy who will someday design the first real Jedi light saber. He'll probably do it. And if he doesn't, someone else will. After all, the world overflows with Lego-like building blocks, available for whatever creations our imaginations might conceive.

Think of today's everyday gadgets that did not even exist one hundred years ago. The achievements of man over the past century boggle the mind. Imagine the reaction of a pre-Industrial Revolution observer, given the chance to catch a glimpse of today's technology. If televisions, telephones, automobiles, airplanes, and indoor toilets don't put him into shock, advances in agriculture, sanitation, and medicine will. Things we take for granted have existed only for a relatively short time—such as immunizations that keep most of our babies alive past age three. Prior generations considered themselves fortunate if half of their children reached adulthood without succumbing to the cruel death of illnesses they couldn't explain, much less cure.

I will never forget the day in 1980 when I was sitting in class as a high school junior and my teacher made a peculiar announcement. He had just read an article suggesting that, in the very near future, home computers were going to become a common household appliance. It should be noted that at the time, "computer" meant that big, dual wheeled machine that school nerds in lab coats spent hours programming in order to print out the most basic calculations. We had no concept of Mac or Microsoft point and click.

The most sophisticated computer game was called "Pong," which featured a tiny blip on the screen hustling back and forth in glorious black and white.

"Why would anyone want a computer in their house?" I mocked with a laugh, unable to grasp what the typical homeowner might do with such a machine or where they would keep the ugly, five-foot-tall contraption.

Within five years, I owned one—and today I have two, not counting the laptop on which I type these words. And just as I could not imagine as a boy what one would do with a home computer, my children cannot imagine what to do without one today. In fact, after informing Shaun that we did not have computers when I was his age, he gave me a perplexed gaze and asked, "Why Dad? Were you poor?"

Legos and computers tell me something important about our Creator. He has an ordered mind. That is why Shaun can create impressive Lego structures and why I can type these words on a laptop. Both the technologies and their use demonstrate a capacity for invention and imagination that God sewed into the fabric of humanity.

By any standard, seventeenth-century mathematician, scientist, and inventor Blaise Pascal ranks among the most brilliant men of the second millennium. Despite his relatively short life—he died at age thirty-nine—his list of accomplishments still impresses. He conducted experiments that laid the foundation for the science of modern hydraulics, developed the first public transportation system in France, and invented the first computer, a mechanical calculator, which served a similar essential function for his time.

Pascal used the order of the world he found to make it a little better, recognizing problems that needed solutions and flaws that needed repair. The most basic flaw he encountered, however, was not man's environment, but man's heart. In his words, "The more enlightened we are, the more greatness and vileness we discover in man."[40] Pascal believed in a God of order, a God who gave mankind the capacity and resources needed to make life better. Greatness. But he also knew that we do much evil. Vileness. We can use the Lego blocks of our world to make computers, but we can also use them to make dirty bombs.

Our world has problems. From the inconvenience of weeds to the tragedy of disease, much wrong needs to be set right. Which is why technology is such a marvel—it enables us to mend what has broken. But there is also much right that can be made wrong. The same know-how that tries to cure cancer is also trying to clone humans. One serves God; the other plays God. While the blocks themselves are neither good nor bad, how we use them reveals us to be, in Pascal's words, either great or vile.

We have invented such marvels as the jumbo jet, X-ray machine, polio vaccine, air conditioner, cellular phone, and automatic garage door opener. A common theme runs through such diverse creations. In a word: redemption. The Lego box allows us to participate in the process of making what is wrong right again, of reaching toward the something better for which we were made, of using the order of things to improve the way of things. And while we will never make life what it should be, we have certainly made it better than it could be, and better than it once was.

I nearly failed geometry during my sophomore year of high school. I never got the process, or purpose, of proving triangles. In my mind, it seemed obvious by looking whether a shape was a triangle. Anyway, somehow I survived the course. English, on the other hand, was a breeze. And so, here I sit today, an adult who cannot prove a triangle. But I can string words together to make a coherent sentence. Those who thrived in geometry and other advanced math classes became engineers designing planes. And so I ride their planes, grateful for the order of math. And they read my books (so I hope), grateful for the order of language. Either way, progress requires order.

If two plus two didn't always equal four, then life would become chaotic. There would be no basic building blocks necessary for radios to function, jets to fly, phones to call, or the Dow to rise. In short, if the Legos didn't fit together, nothing would get done.

A day at the Henry Ford Museum in Dearborn, Michigan, is like a journey through the history of the Industrial Revolution. Using a portion of his vast wealth, Henry Ford accumulated a remarkable assortment of machines—from early household appliances, such as potbellied stoves and hand-powered clothes washers, to heavy farm equipment and steam engine trains. As one would expect, the museum also includes an impressive collection of automobiles, including nineteenth-century single-seat vehicles and the infamous Model T. The various displays serve as successful reminders of how much progress humans made during an era when machines provided the focal point of technological innovation. The cumulative impact can be summarized in one phrase: "We've come a long way, baby!"

The same can be said of a day visiting the Smithsonian Air and Space Museum. The history of flight comes to life, from the Wright Brothers' Kitty-Hawk miracle to Charles Lindberg's Atlantic crossing to Neil Armstrong's giant leap. And all of it occurred in less than a century!

These and other museums point me to the same inkling I find in Shaun's Lego box. An infinite variety of wonders, technologies I will never understand but gladly use, are just waiting to be invented. Thousands of researchers and engineers are working right now to find cures, patent products, and program software that will change the way I live tomorrow. They will fix what is wrong, moving me further from the vile I need repaired toward the great I was made to be. And all of it because the world in which we live—like the God who made it—is one of order.

INKLING

Human innovation reflects a God of order.

CHAPTER FIFTEEN

Do-gooders

When I do good I feel good.
When I do bad I feel bad. And that's my religion.

Christopher Reeve

I knew I had to volunteer for some-
thing. The head of my son's Cub Scout troop said that sign-up
sheets near the door described all the events requiring parental
coordination and that every parent was expected to pitch in. I
wanted to be among the first to choose. If you wait too long, you
might be left with the dregs, like roadside cleanup duty. So while
the other parents listened to an air force pilot talk to the kids, I
moseyed on over to scope out my options.

There must have been twenty or thirty different events from
which to choose, most of which fell outside my schedule or my skill
set. I had not been a scout very long as a boy, so events like knot
tie demonstration or pinewood derby judging lay way outside my
comfort zone. I shuddered at the thought of my ten-year-old son
hanging his head in shame as Dad messed up a slipknot in front of
his entire troop. No sir, I was going to find something for which I
had a knack. Something within my limited repertoire of scouting
experience. And most importantly, something with which my wife
could help me. Fortunately, I found just the thing: Nursing Home
Christmas Caroling.

I remember participating in similar events as a kid, sometimes with a scout troop, other times with a church group. I never liked it. The unpleasant sights and smells of the home often felt a bit scary. God built little boys for hiking and building, not being hugged or yelled at by old ladies they've never met or accidentally glancing through an open door while singing "Away in a Manger" to see a bedpan being changed. So I had some idea what my son and his troop might be feeling about the idea. But it showed up on the list of good deeds for that year. And since it had to be done, I figured I might as well be the one to lead it.

I'm not sure the old folks enjoy the event any more than the kids. Have you ever heard young boys muddle their way through Christmas carols? Great songs of celebration and adoration, hymns the older generation have loved for a lifetime, get butchered beyond recognition. I am certain the Girl Scout performance receives far better marks for musical achievement. (The girls are probably better huggers too.) Still, the event rates as a success by my standards so long as none of the cubs pull the fire alarm or have a wheelchair race down the hallway. In the end, a good deed gets done—which is the whole point.

My son and his fellow cubs will have other opportunities for kindness throughout the year. They can earn patches for picking up trash or mowing someone's lawn or even the cliché gesture of helping old ladies across the street. In so doing, they live up to their pledge to honor God. They also make their little corner of the world better than it was and feel better about themselves for having done so.

Christopher Reeve must have been a scout in his younger years. Once famous for his big-screen portrayal of every boy's hero, Superman, Reeve made us believe he could leap buildings in a single bound and run faster than a locomotive. More recently, his fame has come from an inability even to walk. Victim of a tragic horse-riding accident, Christopher Reeve has spent most of the last decade as a quadriplegic. As a result, he has become Hollywood's patron saint for the disabled, an icon of courage when one loses his or her superhuman powers.

In his autobiographical book, *Nothing Is Impossible,* Reeve reveals a bit about his own search for God. Viewing the traditional view of God as a bit disturbing, in part due to his relationship with his own father, Christopher embraced the Church of Scientology. After fabricating a prior life story that the church accepted as authentic, his skepticism caused him to look elsewhere. He didn't return to traditional religion and what he describes as its effort to "manipulate behavior"—by which one must assume he means the promise to reward good and punish evil. And so, after a long search, Reeve and his family became part of the Unitarian movement, a fairly generic brand of spirituality. "Over the years," he says, "I have come to believe that spirituality is found in the way we live our daily lives. . . . It's not so hard to imagine that there is some kind of higher power. We don't have to know what form it takes or exactly where it exists; just to honor it and try to live by it are enough."[41]

For him, the bottom line of religion is pretty straightforward. He claims the philosophy of fellow do-gooder Abraham Lincoln as his own. In Lincoln's words, "When I do good I feel good. When I do bad I feel bad. And that's my religion."[42]

Like the rest of us, Reeve senses that doing good deeds, however defined, makes us feel closer to God. For him, that means raising the spirits of and funds for the disabled. For me, it means leading a group of boys in botched Christmas carols for the elderly. For both of us, I think it means earning some sort of patch.

~⊙~

Every time I drive past the four-story hospital in our town, I recall how much "do-gooding" I take for granted. Today, when one of my loved ones becomes ill, I can take them to receive top-notch medical attention. It was not always so. Once upon a time, no such places existed. The ancient Roman Empire displayed a harsh indifference to the suffering of the weak and sick. Only the religious motivation of early Christians created the first hospitals in the mid-fourth century.

The same can be said of my local library or college campus. In a time when godless barbarians burned books in Rome, religious monks in Ireland followed the lead of a missionary named Patrick and so preserved the canon of Western knowledge. They wanted to know more of their God and the world he had made, so they celebrated learning.

Picking up trash by the side of the road provides a fitting tribute to Francis of Assisi, often considered the patron saint of environmentalism. He came on the scene at a time when "naturalism" had all but destroyed nature. While pagans worshiped the made rather than the Maker, Francis reintroduced a healthy reverence for creation. In his view, man was not made to serve nature, but to serve God. Francis saw all things as sacred because God made them. He perceived the halo on the edge of all earthly things and reminded man of his God-ordained duty toward the environment.[43]

Much of the fruit we call good deeds grows from the root of religious belief. Even those with no particular faith creed find themselves compelled toward some sort of decency. And so they participate (or at least feel guilty when they don't). In big and small ways, we all do something we consider good because we want to fix what we consider bad.

We volunteer at a soup kitchen to help the poor because we believe some are victims rather than bums.

We serve in the children's ministry at church because we believe it is good to teach kids right from wrong.

To help heal, we build and staff hospitals and give to Jerry Lewis telethons.

We recycle to save the ozone and donate to save the whales.

An interesting trend has appeared among college students today, including those who reject formal religion. One college freshman I'll call Brad, for example, just started at an expensive and rigorous Ivy League university. Brad, who claims no faith, has a partial scholarship requiring five hours per week of community service. He accepted a position helping asthmatic children participate in sports at the local YMCA. You would think Brad would resent the job. After all, he needs to protect his time for study and earning money to pay tuition. But he doesn't. In fact, he feels excited about the role. I guess Brad, like Christopher Reeve, has a religion. He feels good by doing good.

Why do we all have a compulsion to be do-gooders? Probably it is in response to the heart's unspoken creed.

First, we know we are made for something more. We know we were made to be good and feel most like we should when we do what we ought. Second, we know something is wrong with our world. And third, we are trying to fix things, to make them more like they are supposed to be. We might disagree with one another over what needs to be made right and how. We may argue against or admire another's cause. But the motivation remains the same for all of us. We are trying to make right what we see as wrong.

Whether we think God messed things up or we are cleaning up our own mess, we want to earn whatever patches get distributed in the here and now or will be given in the hereafter.

And so, we do good—sometimes in the most unlikely of circumstances.

Private Walter T. Bromwich saw it even in war. A soldier on the front lines of World War I, Bromwich found himself face-to-face with horrific evil—and questioned the God who would allow such devastation. We know of his struggle through a brief letter written to his small-town pastor back home. He describes himself feeling like a cog in a huge wheel. "The cog may get smashed up," he explains "but the machine goes on. . . . And I can't feel God is in it. How can there be fairness in one man being maimed for life, suffering agonies, another killed instantaneously, while I get out of it safe? Does God really love us individually or does He love His purposes more?"

Despite his struggle, however, Walter does find God in the midst of the worst humanity has to offer. "What I would like to believe is that God is in this war, not as a spectator, but backing up everything that is good in us. He won't work any miracles for us because that would be helping us do the work He's given us to do on our own. I don't know whether God goes forth with armies but I do know that He is in lots of our men or they would not do what they do."[44]

Maybe we do good because a good God is "backing up everything that is good in us." Or perhaps we do so because we sense God feels pleased by our goodness, that he somehow uses us to right what has gone wrong. One thing is clear: we do good to feel close to God—whether we believe in him or not.

INKLING

WHEN WE DO GOOD, WE DO GOD.

PART IV

THE STORIES
WE TELL

We are story people.
We know narratives, not ideas.
That's to your advantage.
You have the best redemption story on the market.

SARAH HINLICKY

CHAPTER SIXTEEN

A Bloody Mess

If there's no infinite God, then there's no virtue either,
and no need of it at all.

FYODOR DOSTOYEVSKY

Widely acclaimed as the greatest novel ever written, *The Brothers Karamazov* is a complex and haunting tale. In it, Fyodor Dostoyevsky uses a story of murder to paint a portrait of nineteenth-century Russian society. On the surface it appears similar to his earlier masterpiece, *Crime and Punishment.* But below the mystery lies a chillingly profound portrayal of how belief affects behavior, for better or worse.

Dostoyevsky creates four main characters, a father and three brothers. The father, Fyodor Pavlovich Karamazov, is a despicable man, consumed with his own gratification and caring little for his family. He is aptly described as muddleheaded, but not because he is stupid. He isn't. Fyodor shows himself quite capable of manipulating others to achieve his ends and to accumulate money. He is, however, quite eccentric—whether real or contrived, it is difficult to say. What is certain is that Fyodor Karamazov is a womanizing, abusive drunk.

Dmitri was born of his first wife; Ivan and Alexei, his second. On one level the three boys reflect three different personalities. On another level, they reflect something else.

Dmitri, the oldest, is a playboy. Like his father, he loves to charm women and enjoy the many sensual pleasures life has to offer. But he and Fyodor hate one another with a passion—constantly at odds over money, or loving the same woman, or any number of disputes. Dmitri represents competition, and therefore a threat, to Fyodor. So Fyodor crushes Dmitri on virtually every battlefront and finds great amusement in a game he invariably wins.

Ivan, the second boy, is the intellectual. He loves listening to himself win a good argument, especially when it comes to religion. Ivan prides himself on accepting the "modern" ideas, including the notion that belief in a good God is mere wishful thinking. It is Ivan who utters the novel's most famous and evocative truth: "If there is no God, then all things are permissible." His monologue on the Grand Inquisitor, in which Ivan condemns God as heartless and the church as power hungry, reflects the spirit of his age among the intellectual elite. And it deeply offends his younger brother.

Alexei, more commonly called Alyosha, is the true believer of the family—a gentle, kind heart who loves Christ and takes seriously his command to love others. Alyosha serves as God's defender and shines the light of grace amid a wickedly dark family.

Dmitri is the unhappy man drowning himself in sensual pleasure. Though not religious, he believes in God and knows right from wrong, so guilt drives him further into despair. Ivan is the arrogant man who rejects God. He tries to take the All-Knowing One's place by becoming a know-it-all. Alyosha is a man who loves God and wants others to do likewise.

A fifth character in the story, the half-witted servant of Fyodor, seems to play an insignificant part. Smerdyakov lives with the father, serving his demands and enduring his abuses. We also learn that he is Fyodor's illegitimate son, an unintended consequence of fun on a sexual playground. Victim of frequent epileptic fits, Smerdyakov lives in the shadow of his more enlightened half siblings. He can't help eavesdropping on their frequent debates and finds himself especially drawn to the eloquence of Ivan—which Ivan finds irritating. "Smerdyakov apparently, God knows why, finally came to consider himself somehow in league, as it were, with Ivan Fyodorovich, always spoke in tones as to suggest that there was already something agreed to and kept secret, as it were, between the two of them."[45]

The inciting incident of the story occurs when the man everyone hates is murdered. Fyodor dies after a dispute with his oldest son over money. Witnesses heard Dmitri threaten his father and storm out of the house, making him the prime suspect. The only potential eyewitness to the murder and theft is the illegitimate half-wit, Smerdyakov. But a fit of epilepsy the evening of the murder prevents his seeing. And so Dmitri is arrested and placed on trial, an apparent open-and-shut case, a man certain to be condemned.

But a dark secret comes to light. Ivan is horrified to learn why and for what purpose Smerdyakov considered him a partner. Dmitri hadn't killed their father in a fit of anger. Smerdyakov had killed him with cold, calculating premeditation. He had faked an epileptic incident and seized the opportunity to implement a plot he had been devising for some time, a plot he conceived in league with Ivan—or so he believed. In the most chilling scene of the novel, Smerdyakov confesses all to his intellectual half brother. But guilt does not motivate the confession. It comes more like a mob hit man seeking affirmation from the Mafia boss.

"It was true what you taught me, sir, because you told me a lot about that then: because if there's no infinite God, then there's no virtue either, and no need of it at all. It was true. That's how I reasoned."

"Did you figure it out for yourself?" Ivan grinned crookedly.

"With your guidance, sir."

Indignant at the notion that he had any part in the murderous act, Ivan seeks to distance himself, refusing his "share" of the stolen money. This puzzles Smerdyakov, who wonders why the man who confidently proclaimed the death of virtue would worry over the death of a worthless man. Why should one who taught that a good God is mere wishful thinking condemn his student for acting upon that view?

"You yourself kept saying then that everything was permitted, so why are you so troubled now, you yourself, sir?"[46]

Ivan, who considered himself wise beyond religious belief, has come face-to-face with the hard implications of his view. Ivan's indignation should be puzzling. Smerdyakov fully accepted the notion that there is no God and, therefore, lost any basis for morality. If one can get away with murder in order to make his life better, why not do it?

After all, the pupil has done as he was taught. And as ought to be, the fittest survived.

⁓⊙⌒

Some time ago the Associated Press released a story about E. Frenkel, one of the former Soviet Union's increasing number of psychics. He claimed that he had successfully used his extraordinary abilities to stop bicycles, automobiles, and streetcars. His next trick would be to stop an oncoming train. He felt confident that his psychic-biological powers would force it to halt. They didn't, and it didn't, and he died instantly.

What we believe shapes what we do, whether actually true or not. In the reality created by E. Frenkel, the train stopped. In the reality created by God, it didn't. He rejected basic laws of physics in favor of his own contrivance. E. Frenkel is dead. The laws are alive and well.

What we believe about God shapes who we are—a reality forcefully portrayed in Dostoyevsky's masterpiece. Ivan loved to talk about a godless universe. But when forced to confront someone who

126

actually believed it, someone who took him seriously, he became frightened. To condemn his pupil amounted to sheer hypocrisy.

Like Ivan, those who reject God among the intellectual elite always try to distance themselves from the simplistic masses. Ivan thought Smerdyakov stupid. He didn't worry about how irreligious theories might influence the half-wit. After all, Ivan absorbed such ideas while maintaining respectability. But his respectable life amounted to a disguise, the mask behind which hid a monstrous reality. It was he who gave the killer validation, or at least permission. Who is more guilty? The hit man taking orders or the Mafia boss giving them?

The elite class looks down its arrogant nose at the destructive lifestyles of their half-witted, undignified pupils. They distance themselves by inverting the motto of hypocrisy, cautioning the masses to "do as we do, not as we say!" But more often than not, the masses take the words of their teachers seriously. And sometimes those words justify murder or suicide.

British psychiatrist Theodore Dalrymple sees these patterns of suicide all too clearly. He treats those at the lowest end of English society, the poor in a slum hospital and a prison. His work has led him to one undeniable conclusion: most social pathology exhibited by the underclass has its origin in ideas that have filtered down from the intelligentsia. His book, *Life at the Bottom,* tells one story after another of those who have killed others or are killing themselves, thanks, he claims, to notions they've learned from the Ivans of their world. Notions that suggest there is no God, no ultimate accountability, no basis for avoiding wrong and choosing right.

> The aim of untold millions is to be free to do exactly as they choose and for someone else to pay when things go wrong. . . . Implicitly they disagree with Bacon's famous dictum that "chiefly the mould of a man's fortune is in his own hands." Instead they experience themselves as putty in the hands of fate.[47]

Dr. Dalrymple points a finger at his colleagues within the intellectual class. They cannot continue to distance themselves from the real-life effect of their views. People suffer and die because they believe lies. Like E. Frenkel, they stand before reality's oncoming train, confident it will stop. Dalrymple is tired of cleaning up the resulting bloody mess.

What we believe of God determines how we live. If Ivan is right that there is no God, then he is right that all things are permissible. And he is wrong to condemn is half-witted brother.

That is not to say, of course, that all who claim belief in God do good. Even followers of my Christian faith carried out the horrors of the Inquisition. But they did so in spite of Christ's teachings, not because of them. Looking at the grand sweep of history, we see that societies that reject or remove God live life at the bottom. According to some worldviews, murder can be forgiven; according to others, it can be justified. As University of Texas professor J. Budziszewski put it, if Christians are to blame for the religious butcheries of the sixteenth century, the humanist is to blame for the secular savageries of the twentieth. "I see your thousand Frenchmen; I raise you a million Chinese."[48]

As the story of *The Brothers Karamazov* comes to a close, Ivan learns that Smerdyakov is dead, hanged at his own hand. Ivan's beliefs have caused his father's murder and brother's suicide. It is somehow fitting that the news comes through Alyosha, the one person in the story who consistently believes in and reflects a loving God. Tormented by the devil of disbelief, Ivan needs comfort, a comfort Alyosha yearns to provide but hasn't the capacity to give.

He was beginning to understand Ivan's illness: "The torments of a proud decision, a deep conscience!" God, in whom Ivan did not believe, and his truth were overcoming his heart, which still did not want to submit.

In the end, Alyosha realizes that his brother must repent his disbelief before it claims another victim: Ivan himself.

> "God will win!" he thought. "[Ivan] will either rise into the light of truth, or . . . perish in hatred, taking revenge on himself and everyone for having served something he does not believe in," Alyosha added bitterly, and again prayed for Ivan.[49]

Ideas have consequences—for better or worse.

INKLING

WITHOUT GOD, LIFE BECOMES A BLOODY MESS.

CHAPTER SEVENTEEN

The Myth of Innocence

"Perhaps there aren't any grownups anywhere."
The fat boy looked startled.

WILLIAM GOLDING, *LORD OF THE FLIES*

No adults survived the plane crash. But if anyone could subsist and establish an ordered protocol while stranded on an uninhabited island, these boys could. After all, they had attended a prestigious British preparatory school as sons of society's elite class.

So begins one of the most powerfully disturbing novels of the twentieth century, William Golding's *Lord of the Flies*.

The first order of business is to elect a leader. Two older boys emerge as clear candidates. Jack, because he demands it. As head boy in the school choir, he has come to expect the reluctant obedience of his fellow singers. The second is Ralph, a tall, attractive boy who displays calm confidence. He had befriended the fat kid with glasses, which reassured the unsettled smaller children. After counting the votes, Ralph is made chief.

At first, the thrill of adventure overcomes fear. Searching the island for fruit, hunting for wild animals, and building a giant bonfire keep the boys happily distracted. They even establish rules mirroring those imposed at school, such as holding the seashell conch when one wishes to speak. But amid their industry and civility there exists a seed of peril, sensed most by the one they call Piggy, the fat boy.

It is Piggy who is panicked after discovering no adults on the island. No one to protect him from the cruel teasing and threats that typified his childhood.

It is Piggy who becomes the tribe's object of ridicule, due to his portly shape, weak disposition, and large spectacles.

And it is Piggy who gets tormented most when Jack leads a revolt against the orderly command of Chief Ralph, targeting the weak to appear strong.

The conflict culminates in a deeply troubling scene in which Jack's savage rebels chide Ralph and his few remaining loyalists. As the two wrestle for supremacy, Piggy clutches the conch and pleads with the taunting boys to come to their senses.

"Which is better," he yells up from the rocky cliff, "to be a pack of painted Indians like you are, or to be sensible like Ralph is?"

But they aren't listening, wildly screaming to drown out the lonely voice below.

"Which is better—to have rules and agree, or to hunt and kill?"

They continue to shout, raucously waving their spears.

"Which is better, law and rescue, or hunting and breaking things up?"

Those were Piggy's last words. Jack's warriors shove a large rock over the cliff's edge. As intended, the impact crushes the fat boy's skull and deposits his body into its ocean grave. The weakest link is dead. Even Ralph's noble strength could not protect him. Now, only the fit survive.

The wild screaming fades into stunned silence as all stare in disbelief at what has happened. Ralph, once chief, is now the sole outcast. He flees in fear for his own life.

The tribe tracks him in order to inflict Jack's revenge, even lighting a fire to smoke him out of the jungle's protective cover.

Running from his chanting hunters to the point of exhaustion, Ralph reaches the shoreline's dead end. All hope gone, he falls to the ground and begins a cry for mercy.

At that moment, Ralph sees the last thing he expected. Lifting his head, he beholds a naval officer standing on the beach only a few feet beyond. The smoke, intended for Ralph's ruin, had invited rescue.

The scene of a boy pursued by spear-waving child warriors suggested fun and games. "What have you been doing? Having a war or something?"

Ralph just nodded, then wept. As Golding describes the scene:

> The tears began to flow and sobs shook him. He gave himself up to them now for the first time on the island; great, shuddering spasms of grief that seemed to wrench his whole body. His voice rose under the black smoke before the burning wreckage of the island; and infected by that emotion, the other little boys began to shake and sob too. And in the middle of them, with filthy body, matted hair, and unwiped nose, Ralph wept for the end of innocence, the darkness of man's heart, and the fall through the air of the true, wise friend called Piggy.[50]

Golding's tale of battling boys has become an icon of the human experience. Using children—those assumed to possess untarnished innocence—Golding reminds us of our basic nature. While we may have Ralph's capacity for good, seen in our institutions of learning, industry, and healing, we also have a dark side. And like a deeply embedded weed, it needs very little nourishment to grow and bloom into murderous evil.

Lord of the Flies, written in an era deeply marked by World War II, is rich with symbolism. See the irony of children seeking adult protection from one another, only to be rescued by soldiers entangled in the mass destruction of a grown-up war. Observe Piggy, the victim of abuse echoing the tragic experience of European Jews. And of course, witness the heroic Ralph, willing to risk his own life in defense of the weak—much like Allied troops opposing Hitler.

But the most striking symbolism of the novel grows out of its central theme: well-educated children of privilege abruptly transformed from orderly young gentlemen into cruel, man-hunting savages. The story deeply disturbs us because we recognize ourselves in its telling. It tells us that something is wrong not just around us, but within us. We are not the innocent, loving creatures we believe ourselves to be. We are like unruly children who, if not for adult intervention, would destroy themselves.

I'd like to think I would imitate Ralph, bravely defending the weak. But the history of mankind, and even my own childhood, says I am just as likely to side with Jack.

I'd like to believe that my children are born pure and innocent. But I have observed that doing bad comes naturally. They must be taught to do good.

William Golding described his novel as an attempt to trace the defects of society back to the defects of human nature. Can there be any question that those defects exist? How else does one explain well-educated, privileged Germans participating in the systematic murder of millions of European "Piggys"? We know intuitively that just below the surface of our sophisticated decency lurks a monster.

The apostle Paul acknowledged his own internal conflict in a letter written to Christians in Rome. "I don't understand myself at all," he admitted, "for I really want to do what is right, but I don't do it. Instead, I do the very thing I hate. I know perfectly well that what I am doing is wrong, and my bad conscience shows that I agree that the law is good. But I can't help myself, because it is sin inside me that makes me do these evil things."[51] The defects of society can be traced to the defects of human nature.

Lord of the Flies portrays a view of man held by the dominant religions of the West: Judaism, Christianity, and Islam. They describe us as sinful beings, imperfect, fallen, and weak. Man is not completely virtuous, nor completely wicked. He is both—a tarnished beauty, a spoiled good. We are Hyde and Jekyll. We are Jack and Ralph.

As Jack, we push others down in order to rise to the top. As Ralph, we sacrifice our own desires in order to serve the weak.

As Jack, the spark of wildness calls us to decadence. As Ralph, the prick of conscience holds us back.

As Jack, we should be punished. As Ralph, we should be rescued.

Both realities suggest my need for God. I need him to land on my island of turmoil and set things right. I need him to salvage what is decent and subdue what is depraved. Mostly, I need his grace to redeem me back from bad to the good I was made to be.

INKLING

I NEED GOD TO RESCUE ME FROM MYSELF.

CHAPTER EIGHTEEN

A Candle Lit

God bless Us, Every One!

It may just be the most well-known literary work on the planet. And it is only going to become more popular as millions relive the story each December through their television screens.

My personal favorite is the 1951 production starring Alastair Sim. I own the video, along with several others. One stars George C. Scott, another alters the story with Henry Winkler as a Depression-era American miser named Benedict Slade. There is also a wonderful Focus on the Family radio dramatization my family enjoys each year, and a Mickey Mouse animated retelling for the kids. I'm sure there are at least twenty other adaptations that have been brought to life on the big screen, with actors like Bill Murray, and the small screen or stage, with stars like Patrick Stewart. They all are directly or loosely based upon the masterpiece that none surpass or even completely capture: A Christmas Carol by Charles Dickens.

I won't bother retelling the entire story. It is a popular fantasy, with four ghostly visitations to the Christmas-loathing humbug named Ebenezer Scrooge—whom Dickens describes as a "squeezing, wrenching, grasping, scraping, clutching, covetous, old sinner."[52] But by the end, the Scrooge everyone fears and despises gets transformed into "as good a friend, as good a master, and as good a man, as the good old city knew, or any other good old city, town, or borough, in the good old world."[53] And that, at the core, is why we love it so much. Scrooge One makes us frown while Scrooge Two makes us smile. We know how the story ends, yet we enjoy watching the transformation year after year after year. Why is that, and what does it tell us of God?

Scrooge One is a man who, if possible, seems happy in his misery (or at least content there). He seems unaware and unconcerned that he emanates the darkness of hell, even as those around him bask in the light of heaven. Wealth fails to warm his spirit, as surely as poverty fails to chill theirs. Dickens paints him as a man possessing all of the qualities necessary to repel rather than invite human affection, as if intentionally gathering such traits to himself.

> Hard and sharp as flint, from which no steel had ever struck out generous fire; secret, and self-contained, and solitary as an oyster. The cold within him froze his old features, nipped his pointed nose, shrivelled his cheek, stiffened his gait; made his eyes red, his thin lips blue; and spoke out shrewdly in his grating voice. A frosty rime was on his head, and on his eyebrows, and his wiry chin. He carried his low temperature always about him; he iced his office in the dog days; and didn't thaw it one degree at Christmas.[54]

His cold, prickly shell served its purpose. None stopped to greet him on the street. Beggars knew better than to seek his charity. No children asked him the time. "Even the blind men's dogs appeared to know him;" says Dickens, "and when they saw him coming on, would tug their owners into doorways and up courts; and then would wag their tails as though they said, 'No eye at all is better than an evil eye, dark master!'"[55]

Scrooge One is the kind of person none of us want to know, but all do know. In fact, at certain times and in certain ways, he is someone we all can be. We all hide from those reflecting the warm light of heaven whenever we imprison ourselves in the cold solitude of self-pity or self-hatred. I myself go there from time to time. It is not a place I like to stay long. But I imagine I could grow accustomed to it, perhaps even learn to prefer it. Many do. Scrooge did.

Never is the contrast between chosen darkness and the light of God more evident than when Ebenezer meets the first of three Christmas spirits. Such brightness shone from his aged yet childlike head that Scrooge wished it covered by a cap the ghost carries under his arm. "'What!' exclaimed the Ghost, 'would you so soon put out, with worldly hands, the light I give? Is it not enough that you are one of those whose passions made this cap!'"[56]

Eyes accustomed to darkness abhor bright light. Dark hearts do the same.

Most adventure tales feature a virtuous hero forced to leave the comforts of a nice life to confront and overcome the perils of evil—perhaps to free a captured friend or lover. In this story, the model gets turned on its head. Ebenezer is jerked from a loathsome existence to face the perils of good. Instead of winning the day, he gets soundly defeated by an enemy who pries freedom's key from Scrooge's tightly clutched fist. Once released, the prison cell opens, inviting him to leave its shadowy coldness and enter the warm brightness of the light beyond. The joy he so jealously guarded himself against finally invades his pale existence. The crooked wick of Ebenezer's candle is finally lit.

And what a lighting! Literally overnight, a hard, miserly Mr. Scrooge becomes the lovable, generous Uncle Ebenezer. After dragging the reader through the journey of Scrooge One in 95 percent of the story, Dickens finally makes it all worthwhile by introducing Scrooge Two. It doesn't take long. We get only a few snapshots of what can happen when light overtakes darkness, as when he dances in the bedroom upon realizing he hasn't missed Christmas.

> "I don't know what to do!" cried Scrooge, laughing and crying in the same breath. "I am as light as a feather, I am as happy as an angel, I am as merry as a schoolboy. I am as giddy as a drunken man. A merry Christmas to everybody!"[57]

Or turning a child into coconspirator by sending the prize turkey to Bob Cratchit's home.

> "Go and buy it, and tell 'em to bring it here, that I may give them the direction where to take it. Come back with the man, and I'll give you a shilling. Come back with him in less than five minutes and I'll give you half-a-crown!"[58]

Or shocking the skeptical charity director by making a sizable donation to the poor.

> "Not a farthing less. A great many back-payments are included in it, I assure you."

Or playfully scaring his tardy employee at work the following morning.

> "I am not going to stand this sort of thing any longer. And therefore, I am about to raise your salary! I'll raise your salary, and endeavor to assist your struggling family, and we will discuss your affairs this very afternoon, over a Christmas bowl of smoking bishop, Bob! Make up the fires, and buy another coal-scuttle before you dot another i, Bob Cratchit!"[59]

Just a few scenes, but enough to let us know a candle now shines because a man has been transformed. Despite his miserable past, or maybe because of it, the story has a happy ending. His is a tale of redemption—of sudden, unexpected joy. My ability to identify with Scrooge's prison lets me share in the delight of his release.

It creates a lump in my throat and melts my spirit like frost-nipped hands before a blazing fireplace.

~⚭~

Have you ever noticed that virtually every religion links solving humanity's problem with the concept of light? Eastern faiths and New Age gurus, for example, invite us to embrace higher consciousness through "enlightenment" so that we can rise above the darkness of ignorance.

Jews light candles to reflect a God whom the Torah describes synonymously as "my light" and "my salvation." They also celebrate the Law, which is called "a lamp unto my feet and a light unto my path."

Catholics do the same because Jesus claimed to be "the light of the world." Protestants don't light as many candles, because some don't want to appear Catholic. But we all hang Christmas lights, in part to impress the neighbors. We also do it because the Bible tells us "God is light, and in him is no darkness at all." Christ commanded us, "Let your light so shine before men."

Even those who reject formal religion associate solutions with light and problems with darkness. We "shed light on the subject" in order to dispel ignorance. We celebrate the "Enlightenment" for bringing us out of the so-called "Dark Ages." We smile to brighten someone's day. We sit in dark rooms when depressed.

Light is a universal symbol of good. We even draw hope from dying people who claim to see a bright light. We don't know the source of that light. They could just as easily be peering into the scorching flames of hell as the warm glow of heaven. But deep down we sense that light implies good, something to welcome, while darkness suggests bad, something to avoid. I have yet to meet a child afraid of the light.

Light is more powerful than darkness. You can light more candles, but you can't turn up the dark. Darkness is a negation, defined by what isn't rather than what is.

Some words we easily associate with darkness, such as hate, greed, and fear. Scrooge One lived in their shadow. Others fall in the category of light, like love, kindness, and hope. Scrooge Two basked in their glow. My favorite word is another in light's column: the word *redemption*. Redemption bridges the chasm between warm and cold, bright and dull, joy and sorrow, Scrooge One and Scrooge Two. It makes wrong right again, rescues us from darkness and places us in the light. And thankfully, it is a word God loves putting to use.

No matter how many times or ways I enjoy the tale, *A Christmas Carol* prompts an overwhelming urge to smile at what the story reflects and invites. It reminds me that God can invade the deepest darkness and warm the coldest heart. It tells me that he can even rescue me from the prison of things I most desire, freeing me to reflect rather than extinguish heaven's light. And, as Tiny Tim observed, it shouts the good news of redemption by declaring, "God bless Us, Every One!" Indeed. He has.

INKLING

GOD IS THE LIGHT OF LIFE.

CHAPTER NINETEEN

Redemption

You belong no longer to evil, but to good.
It is your soul that I am buying for you.

BISHOP BIENVENU

I had previously seen two other Broadway shows: *Seven Brides for Seven Brothers* and *The Phantom of the Opera.* Both were fantastic, so I expected no less from this one.

I saw *Seven Brides* in Detroit when I was seventeen, trying to impress a girl by bringing her to the live performance of her all-time favorite movie. She was impressed—by the show more than by me. I saw *Phantom* in Los Angeles with another girl when I was twenty-six—I took my wife to celebrate our fifth wedding anniversary. The two experiences could not have been more different. *Seven Brides* was playful and light; *Phantom,* intense and dark. Date one ended with a handshake. Date two ended with, well, something better.

And now, after years of hearing that we simply had to see *Les Miserables* on stage, opportunity knocked. The tour had reached Denver, an hour drive from our home. So as soon as my wife and I heard the first advertisement, we called for tickets. I had not yet read the book but knew the basic story thanks to a recent film version. I purchased a souvenir program in the lobby and thumbed through it while waiting for the show to begin.

I learned that Victor Hugo was to nineteenth-century France what Charles Dickens was to England and Leo Tolstoy to Russia. His earlier works included a touching tragedy titled *The Hunchback of Notre Dame*, making him France's greatest living writer by the age of thirty. In 1845, he began a sixteen-year labor writing what became his masterpiece, *Les Miserables*.

While watching what promoters call "the world's most popular musical," I fell in love with the story. I later devoured the book and asked my creative team to produce our own radio theatre adaptation starring England's Brian Blessed and Geoffery Palmer. Not an easy task considering the size and complexity of the book! Our version, like others, required careful scene selection in order to capture the essence of the story. We had no questions, however, about the opening scene.

Jean Valjean has spent the past nineteen years in prison after stealing a loaf of bread to feed his sister's starving family. Now the real struggle begins, moving from town to town, pleading for work. No one will help, frightened off by the color of his passport, which tells them Valjean is a very dangerous "ex-convict." Hunger had led him to imprisonment. Prison released him to hunger once again.

Enter Bishop Bienvenu, a compassionate priest who invites Jean Valjean in from the cold to enjoy a hot meal and warm bed for the night. Unlike others, Bienvenu shows no sign of fear. He seems unconcerned for personal safety. Instead, his concern focuses on one of God's children whose life has been shattered by a misery that ought not be. Thus was his nature. "He inclined towards the distressed and the repentant," says Hugo. "The universe appeared to him like a vast disease; he perceived fear everywhere . . . the whole world was to this good and rare priest a permanent subject of sadness seeking to be consoled."

Though free from chains, Valjean is hunted by the ruthless masters of anger, hatred, and a cancerous craving to exact revenge upon a cruel world. Sensing the pursuit, Bishop Bienvenu intervenes. "You need not tell me who you are," he tells the hunted.

> "This is not my house; it is the house of Christ. It does not ask any comer whether he has a name, but whether he has an affliction. You are suffering; you are hungry and thirsty; be welcome. . . . This is the home of no man, except him who needs an asylum. I tell you, who are a traveler, that you are more at home here than I; whatever is here is yours. What need have I to know your name? Besides, before you told me, I knew it. . . your name is my brother."[60]

Bienvenu escorts Jean Valjean to the guest room where the clergyman invites his guest to sleep on clean sheets and a mattress for the first time in nearly twenty years. Such kindness makes Valjean uncomfortable. Why would the poor bishop share so generously? Why doesn't this defenseless man fear the danger posed? Why would a compassionate priest call a hardened convict his brother? Valjean feels shaken. His misery has been invaded.

Later that night, Valjean flees the priest's home. Before leaving, he steals the silver table settings from the cupboard to sell for much needed cash. The authorities catch him the next morning. As they drag him back to Bienvenu's door, he claims the items were a gift from the priest. While justice demanded restitution and punishment, grace had a different plan. As the undeniably guilty convict's eyes meet the bishop's, the invasion intensifies.

"Ah, there you are!" the bishop said, looking at Valjean. "I am glad to see you. But! I gave you the candlesticks also, which are silver like the rest, and would bring two hundred francs. Why did you not take them along with your plates?"

The astonished guards wondered whether Valjean may have been telling the truth—but Valjean felt even more astonished. As the bishop handed the candlesticks to the thief-turned-recipient, Bienvenu drew near and finalized the invasion in a low voice:

"Forget not, never forget that you have promised me to use this silver to become an honest man. . . . Jean Valjean, my brother: you belong no longer to evil, but to good. It is your soul that I am buying for you. I withdraw it from dark thoughts and from the spirit of perdition, and I give it to God!"[61]

Misery and the bitterness it spawns had been defeated. Good and the hope it instills had won. Evil's hunt had ceased, overtaken by the Hound of Heaven.

The rest of Valjean's story could be summarized in a single word: redemption. He did become an honest man and used the gifted silver to fund a new identity and life. Rather than seeking to avenge his suffering, he sought to relieve the suffering of others, most dramatically an impoverished prostitute named Fantine and an abused orphan girl named Cosette. His life began to reflect its new master. Once owned by evil, his soul had been redeemed by good. The God who seemed so merciless and callous suddenly revealed his true form. A world of laws that only condemned suddenly knew the invasion of grace. All because Jean Valjean experienced a greater reality uttered by the impoverished priest who had changed his life. "God is more than just."[62]

Of all the stories we tell, few satisfy the heart's deepest yearning for God as powerfully as *Les Miserables*. Chiefly because it gives us hope that God can invade our darkest misery and redeem the bad to good. Victor Hugo knew that we are made for more, that something is wrong, and that it needs to be made right again. He also knew that God must do the right-making.

Deep within every human soul lives a desire for justice. We want those who wrong us to pay—often to the point that a desire for retribution or revenge consumes us, like it did Valjean. On one level, this is fitting. Without the rule of law, society descends into chaos. Without punishment, ultimate justice goes begging. Jean Valjean's nemesis in the story, Inspector Javert, personifies the cold, hard requirements of justice. His endless pursuit of Valjean reveals a system with no room for sympathy or the mercy it stirs. "If you break the law, you will be found and punished. No questions asked. No excuses heard."

We all want justice. That is, until we find ourselves its prey.

Other inklings tell me that if God is only love, he isn't enough. But if God is justice only, I'm not enough. Nearly every religion assumes a God who expects us to behave ourselves. Of course, that is the problem. Whether a harsh world has twisted my desire for good or my twisted heart has created a harsh world, I don't behave myself. Nor do you. None of us go through life untouched by the bad both around us and within us. Our world is not as it should be. Neither are we. As I see it, either God is setting us up for failure or setting up a surprise twist in the story.

The surprise twist, of course, is invasion. When all seems dark, light breaks through. Where misery rules, joy occupies. The best moment of the stories we love occurs when the lonely guy finally gets the lovely girl, when the cavalry rides in to save the day at the darkest possible moment, or when the virtuous hero committed to good defeats the sinister villain bent on evil. Contrary to popular belief, we do not love happy endings because we are trying to escape reality. We love happy endings because we are trying to connect with it!

Les Miserables offers hope by reminding me that ultimate reality includes a God who is more than justice. Frankly, I embrace the Christian faith because it points to a God who expects us to behave ourselves but who also knows we can't. He is not the callous Inspector Javert who wants to convict and imprison the criminal, but the compassionate Bishop Bienvenu who wants to buy him back to good. Yes, God is in the business of justice. But he is also in the business of redemption.

INKLING

GOD IS MORE THAN JUST.

CHAPTER TWENTY

Contact

Is anybody out there?

Ellie Arroway

Only four or five times in my life have I walked out of a movie theater feeling a sense of amazement. Amazed by the spectacular special effects I had just seen. Amazed by the profound implications of the story. And amazed by the off-screen drama that must have preceded the one on-screen.

Contact amazed me.

The 1997 film is based upon the book of the same title published more than a decade earlier. Significant differences exist between the two versions—there usually are when Hollywood adapts a story to fit the limitations and potential of the big screen. But this provides one of those rare instances when, in my view, the adapters actually improved the story. Carl Sagan wrote a novel only a scientist could love, complete with more technical details than most care to know. Still, the book is worth the effort for those willing to endure stretches of tedium. The film, on the other hand, moves along quickly, thanks to a director who won a few creative wrestling matches with the author. It paid off in what became a powerful and entertaining movie.

The opening scene marks a stunning achievement for computer generation, convincing the eye that it is traveling through the cosmos. On a journey with sound waves launched from Earth, you move out farther and farther into space, passing every planet before leaving our solar system, which shrinks to a small subsystem of the Milky Way—itself becoming a tiny member of a vast network of galaxies. Within seconds you see galaxies absorbed into greater constellations until what we consider immense appears microscopic. Not even two minutes into the film, and you have experienced the reality of just how small you are!

The story opens with a very intelligent nine-year-old girl who is consumed by a passion to make contact, starting with ham radio buffs a thousand miles south. Ellie Arroway adores her widowed father. When asked whether he thinks people on other planets might exist, he feeds her obsession. "If it is just us," he says with a twinkle in his eye, "it seems like an awful waste of space." When asked whether he thinks Ellie's radio could reach her deceased mother, he dispels any seed of faith. "I don't think even the biggest radio could reach that far." Like her beloved daddy, Ellie dreams of life on other planets—but not life after death. Hers will be a universe defined by material rather than spiritual realities.

Decades later, we meet Ellie as Dr. Arroway, a woman consumed by a passion to make contact, to discover intelligent life beyond Earth. Despite the ridicule of peers for using her considerable gifts to chase after "little green men," Ellie spends years looking and listening for any trace of distant neighbors. One day, that search pays off. She hears a message that must indicate intelligent life. The form of the message is mathematical, the only truly universal language. The substance of the message surpasses her wildest imagining. Someone has sent instructions for building a machine that will transport one human being into space and enable face-to-face communication, face-to-face contact.

Events unfold rapidly. World leaders fund the machine's development. A panel of representatives screen potential candidates for the trip. Ellie makes the short list and appears the sure choice. But when asked about her spiritual beliefs, she confesses that she does not believe in God and that she cannot represent the majority population who believe in some sort of supreme being. Authorities pass over Ellie because, in the words of friend and panel member Palmer Joss, "I just couldn't in good conscience vote for a person who doesn't believe in God. Someone who honestly thinks the other ninety-five percent of us suffer from some sort of mass delusion."

Ellie had accused Palmer, a popular spiritual leader, of believing in God because he needed to believe it. She pointed to a scientific principle known as Occam's Razor, that all things being equal, the simplest explanation tends to be the right one. Ellie found it hard to believe that a mysterious, all-powerful God created everything but left no proof of his existence. It seemed simpler, in her mind, to believe that "we created him so as not to feel so small."

In the end, however, fortunes change. The first attempt fails due to a crazed religious zealot who condemns the entire scientific establishment for meddling in matters that belong to the sphere of faith. His followers mindlessly chant "Praise God" while waving signs that read, "Science is not our God." Their leader literally calls down fire from heaven by strapping a bomb to himself and destroying both the transport and its team. Now the way opens for Ellie to go.

Her trip furnishes us with another stunning film sequence. Ellie feels overcome with emotion as she journeys to distant places more beautiful than words can describe. "I had no idea," comes her awestruck response. "No words. . . . They should have sent a poet."

In those few dramatic moments, Ellie encounters something profound. "For as long as I can remember," she says, "I've been searching for something, some reason why we're here. What are we doing here? Who are we?" Her search ends.

Back home, Ellie finds herself with no evidence of the trip or the things she saw. She has to describe an experience that she cannot prove but that has changed her forever. Hard questions come, very much like the ones she had asked religious friends whom she considered mere wishful thinkers. "You come to us with no evidence, no records, no artifacts. Only a story that, to put it mildly, strains credibility. . . . Are you really going to sit there and tell us we should just take this all on faith?"

Ellie's tearful response fails to satisfy those at her inquiry but touches a deep longing of those in the film audience—words that just as easily could be heard in a hanky-waving, revival tent meeting.

> "I had an experience. I can't prove it. I can't even explain it. But everything that I know as a human being, everything that I am tells me that it was real. I was given something wonderful, something that changed me forever. A vision of the universe that tells us undeniably how tiny and insignificant and how rare and precious we all are. A vision that tells us that we belong to something that is greater than ourselves and that none of us are alone. I wish I could share that. I wish that everyone, if even for one moment, could feel that awe and humility and hope."[63]

Ellie's testimony mixes such emotion with spirituality that you can almost hear the crowd shouting back at her, "Amen, sister. Amen."

When I was a kid, I loved watching *Lost in Space*. Nearly every episode included a scene where the bubble-headed robot waved his accordion tube arms while shouting, "Danger, Will Robinson. Danger!" at the sight of approaching aliens. As a teenager I gravitated toward *Close Encounters of the Third Kind* or the harmless adventure of an odd-looking little guy named ET who wanted to phone home. In recent years we enjoyed the eerie mysteries of the *X-Files*, a series that gives one the sense that Area 54 and alien abductions might just be more than fiction. An irreverently wacky show called *Third Rock from the Sun* gives one the sense those aliens might not be so frightening after all.

For as long as I can remember, mankind has felt fascinated by the idea of alien beings making contact with us or us them. Be it *Star Trek* or *Star Wars,* we have enjoyed fantasizing about what and who might be out there—taking comfort in or scaring ourselves with the notion that we might not be alone in the universe. Like young Ellie Arroway, we want an answer to the nagging question, "Is anybody out there?"

Carl Sagan wrote *Contact.* Fitting, since the die-hard skeptic pioneered exploring the possibility that life on earth originated on another planet. After decades of trying to explain the wonder of our cosmos without its Maker, he eventually became like the mindless religious fanatics he considered intolerable. Sagan could no more bear the idea that we are alone than anyone else, to the point that he embraced an idea far less science than it is science fiction.

He's not alone. A growing field of study in the scientific community called Directed Panspermia postulates that life was originally "planted" on Earth from another planet. After years observing the incredible complexity of life and codiscovering the genetic software commonly called DNA, 1962 Nobel Prize winner Dr. Francis Crick finally threw up his hands trying to make what he observed line up with the theory that life spontaneously evolved. He described the improbabilities as so staggering it seemed more likely that life arrived here from outer space. I guess Sagan's novel was his way of shouting back, "Amen, brother, Amen."

I don't mean to belittle Sagan, Crick, or other scientists trying to find intelligent life in outer space. They simply want an answer to the question we all ask: "Is anybody out there?" But as they busy themselves listening for a distant message that may never come, they ignore a message so close that it can be heard every moment of every day. The heavens indeed declare the glory of God. So does the wind and the water and DNA.

I try to help my children observe the tangible evidences of unseen realities. Ultimate acceptance of God requires faith, but not blind faith. I want them to experience what we believe as reasonable. "How could God be real if we can't see him?" I ask my then five-year-old Kyle.

"That's a good question, Dad!" he responds.

"Well, is there anything else we know is real but we can't see?" I ask.

Gravity and sound waves make the list, illustrated by jumping off a chair and turning on the stereo.

"How about air?" suggests Mom, prompting me to pull out several balloons.

"Air is real enough to expand these balloons. I bet air has power too," I say while releasing the balloon. We spend the next ten minutes in intense competition to see who can make his balloon fly farthest. After the fun, we memorize a little jingle that Kyle and my other children remember years later: "Just like air, God is there."

Imbedded into the fabric of our universe lies a simple message. We are not alone. Somebody is out there. He can't be seen. But then, neither can the gravity keeping our feet on the ground or the air giving our lungs what we need to survive. The message seems so simple to a five-year-old—so why does it appear so hard for the rest of us? Perhaps because we have never truly embraced Occam's Razor.

William of Occam was a fourteenth-century philosopher and theologian who developed a principle that underlies all scientific modeling and theory building. Ellie Arroway summarized his emphasis well: All things being equal, the simplest explanation tends to be the right one. In other words, keep it simple, stupid. His work on knowledge, logic, and scientific inquiry played a major role in the transition from medieval to modern thought because he based scientific knowledge on experience and self-evident truths.

William of Occam was a deeply religious man who worshiped a God of order, a God who created a world that follows certain rules. That world, he surmised, could therefore be deciphered. Thus, Occam planted a seed that would bloom into centuries of scientific exploration and discovery.

I wonder how William would react to a story like *Contact*. What might he say to those who claim his principle yet ignore its foundation? How would he respond to people desperately reaching for some sort of transcendence and awe, to the point of accepting notions anything but simple and that Sagan himself admitted have no evidence?

Contact cannot escape suspicion number one. We know we are made for more. While we don't want to be top dog, we yearn for something bigger than ourselves. Having grown too big for our britches, we want to be small again. We want to be put in our place, perhaps so that we know we have one.

All things being equal, the simplest explanation is still the best one.

INKLING

JUST LIKE AIR, GOD IS THERE.

PART V

THE RELIGIONS
WE PROFESS

I see that in every way you are very religious.

THE APOSTLE PAUL

CHAPTER TWENTY-ONE

The New Athens

All the religions are spread before me,
a great spiritual smorgasbord,
and I'll help myself, thank you.

FRANK MCCOURT

The cover story displayed an odd-looking child. At first glance, I thought him a miniature Buddha. Upon closer examination, however, I noticed a yarmulke on his head (that saucerlike cap worn by devout Jewish men) and several emblems around his neck: a cross, the half-moon of Islam, as well as a black and white Ying Yang symbol. Splashed over his image appeared the theme of this particular issue of the *Utne Reader*, a leading alternative media publication: "Designer God: In a mix-and-match world, why not create your own religion?"

The feature article, "God with a Million Faces," describes what critics call "cafeteria religion" as perhaps the truest spiritual quest of all. Author Jeremiah Creedon writes:

A friend of mine I'll call Anne-Marie is the founder of a new religious faith. Like other belief systems throughout the ages, the sect of Anne-Marie exists to address life's most haunting questions. If I ask her why we're born and what happens when we die, her answers suggest that our time on earth has meaning and purpose. Whether I buy it hardly matters. The sect of Anne-Marie has one member, Anne-Marie, and that's plenty.

But, as the writer explains, Anne-Marie's personal religion did not begin with a voice from the sky revealing God's mind. In fact, there is nothing really original about it at all. That's because it kind of accumulated over time by grabbing bits and pieces from this and that faith.

> An artist by trade, Anne-Marie has turned her spirituality into a creative act. Her beliefs are drawn from many sources, some ancient, some new. When Anne-Marie speaks of karma and reincarnation, I hear the influence of Hinduism and Buddhism. Her sense that certain places in nature are sacred is either as new as deep ecology or as old as Shinto. It's hard to say exactly how quantum physics fits into the picture, but she says it does. Beneath it all lies the ethical lexicon of her Christian upbringing, timeworn but still discernible, like the ruins of a Spanish mission.[64]

When asked why she left her girlhood church, Anne-Marie gets blunt. "I needed beliefs that empower me, and organized religion is disempowering," she says. "It's bogus." Anne-Marie's viewpoint appeared in the alternative press, but it reflects an increasing mainstream trend.

Not long ago, in fact, God made the cover of the very mainstream *Life* magazine. I'm sure it was no big deal to him, but it caught my eye. In large black letters, the magazine posed a question: "When you think of GOD what do you see?" Inside appears an essay and photo gallery highlighting major and minor faith groups in America, including Jews, Hindus, Muslims, Mormons, Catholics, Protestants, Buddhists, and several less familiar sects.

The essay comes from the pen of Frank McCourt, wildly successful author of the *New York Times* best-selling book, *Angela's Ashes,* a memoir detailing his struggles growing up poor and Catholic in Ireland. This article, like that book, bleeds leftover angst from a man angry with a religious dad who drank his paycheck despite sick and hungry kids—and at a God who would let it happen. McCourt speaks for many who left the church after trying unsuccessfully to reconcile the beliefs of the faithful with their behavior. In his words:

> So I wrote a book and when I go around the country talking about it people ask me if I'm still Catholic. Well . . . in a way I am. I drop in to churches. I talk to Saint Francis of Assisi and Teresa of Avila, my favorites. I light candles for people's intentions. . . . But I don't confine myself to the faith of my fathers anymore. All the religions are spread before me, a great spiritual smorgasbord, and I'll help myself, thank you.[65]

To be honest, something inside me finds his conclusion appealing. After all, there are so many religions out there—who am I to say one is true and the rest false? Even if I wanted to, how does one sort through the haystack of small "t" truths to find the capital "T" needle? It seems much easier and tolerant to pick-and-choose, mix-and-match, live-and-let-live. Maybe Anne-Marie and Frank McCourt are onto something. Who better to decide what's true for me than me? Besides, aren't we all basically saying the same thing?

But something else inside me finds this mind-set sophomoric. My spiritual quest has brought me face-to-face with irreconcilable differences between religious creeds. Only those who choose to remain ignorant can embrace the notion that Jesus, Buddha, Mohammed, and the Dalai Lama sing different verses to the same song. They don't.

So begins the hard work—examining the core message of each. I can do so with an open mind, assuming all may be partly right. But my heart longs for one to ring entirely true, to completely satisfy its unspoken creed.

⁓◉∽

I consider modern America the new Athens, and my spiritual journey similar to the apostle Paul's stroll through the Greek

Parthenon. The apostle visited Athens as a Roman citizen and a Hellenistic Jew, devout in Judaism but immersed in the wider culture of his time, including a religious pluralism surpassing our own. The Parthenon provided more than a collection of idols and altars, demonstrating the tolerance of a diverse population. It reflected something far more meaningful: the reality and mystery of one true God.

In *The Decline and Fall of the Roman Empire,* historian Edward Gibbon describes an ancient world of "religious harmony" in which most embraced or at least respected each other's superstitions. The intellectual class participated in various rituals and ceremonies not because they were devout, but because they were civil. "The philosopher," he explains "who considered the system of polytheism as a composition of human fraud and error, could disguise a smile of contempt under the mask of devotion without apprehending that either the mockery or the compliance would expose him to the resentment of any invisible or, as he conceived them, imaginary powers."[66] In other words, they participated in the festivals and sacrifices because that's what someone from polite society did.

They could do so, of course, because they did not see mythology as religion. Mythology never wanted to be religion, something many forget. Mythology is the work of an artist telling stories, not a prophet declaring truth. I like G. K. Chesterton's explanation.

> He who has most sympathy with myths will most fully realise that they are not and never were a religion, in the sense that Christianity or even Islam is a religion. They satisfy some of the needs satisfied by a religion; and notably the need for doing certain things at certain dates; the need of the twin ideas of festivity and formality. But though they provide a man with a calendar they do not provide him with a creed.
>
> Certainly a pagan does not disbelieve like an atheist, any more than he believes like a Christian. He feels the presence of powers about which he guesses and invents.

> We know the meaning of all the myths. . . . And it is not the
> voice of a priest or a prophet saying, "These things are." It is the
> voice of a dreamer and an idealist crying, "Why cannot these
> things be?"[67]

In short, mythology represents man's attempt to paint a portrait of a God he imagined, but had never met. Only Jews and Christians—both of whom claimed knowledge of the one true God—stood apart. Paganism was not, in their view, harmless superstition. Jews were forbidden to worship a graven image, while Christians considered demons the authors, patrons, and objects of idolatry.[68]

In this context Paul entered Athens, possessing the background and insight necessary to bridge the gap. A Roman citizen, observant Jew, and Christian apostle—his life brought all three perspectives together. The Greeks had one altar to an unknown god. In truth, says Chesterton, all their gods were unknown gods. "And the real break in history did come when St. Paul declared to them whom they had ignorantly worshiped."[69] Paul offered more than just another mythology among many. He claimed certainty, offering a message that "met the mythological search for romance by being a story and the philosophical search for truth by being a true story."[70] Paul created a crisis for the Roman world when he declared that its mysterious god could be known with certainty. That world was never the same again.

Just as the ancient Greeks brought the best of pagan mythologies together into a single, homogenized system, we have created a spiritual melting pot in America. As it should be, religious freedom means we can choose to believe or not believe whatever we wish. But it also places the burden of decision on every individual. And frankly, many of us are too lazy or intimidated to take that responsibility seriously. Like many Athenians of old, we celebrate uncertainty. We applaud those who offer options and invite us to sample all without taking any seriously—thus placing religion in the same category as party hors d'oeuvres. Nice to have, but not essential. My stroll through the Parthenon of today's religious landscape seems similar to Paul's. Like Athens, I see many spiritual options. People in my day, like some in his, consider any choice equally valid, since none are ultimately true.

But a major and very important difference does exist. Unlike Paul's era, today's major world religions do not see themselves as the work of artistic imagination. They see themselves as the result of divine revelation. They are not seekers asking questions, but rather prophets declaring answers.

Our last set of inklings moves beyond things that my heart senses true in human invention, pain, joy, and stories, to things declared true by religion. Unlike Anne-Marie and Frank McCourt, I refuse to patronizingly consider all faiths equally valid. That only makes them equally false. We may be saying some of the same things. But that does not make us all the same.

We find mankind's common creed in the questions posed, not the answers given. Yes, we all reach for the same God and try to pick the same lock. But as my journey revealed, clearly we are using different keys.

INKLING

GOD CAN BE KNOWN.

CHAPTER TWENTY-TWO

Am I God?

I am God!

SHIRLEY MACLAINE

It seemed an unconventional assignment. My idea of studying other religious perspectives amounted to reading books that would boost my confidence in Christianity by criticizing non-Christian faiths. I never imagined it would mean walking onto their turf to discuss what they believed and why. But my seminary professor had this strange idea that his students needed firsthand, first-person encounters. So, in order to pass his class, I had to conduct an interview with two members of the opposing team. Even more challenging, I had to be nice—listening and learning rather than talking and teaching.

My first encounter occurs in a spiritual community called "Astara" located in Upland, California. I feel conflicted as I walk onto the campus in search of someone to interview. The facilities look inviting, the buildings well kept and the grounds nicely groomed. The layout appears to merge a Baptist Sunday school building and a small private college campus. But the tranquility of the environment fades as I read the brochure describing the kinds of "spiritual exploration" hosted here.

People from all faiths study esoteric teachings and mystic philosophy through Astara. You may maintain membership in any religion and still become an Astarian. This is a way to explore life's most personal and meaningful treasures. If you want the mystical wisdom of the ages, if you want to express hidden potentials of mind and Higher Self, you may be very near the answers to your desires. If you seek enlightenment, healing for body and soul, new inspiration and aspiration, you may find the realization of your personal goals and dreams through Astara, a place of light, a lodestar on the true path of the soul.[71]

It invites me to embark upon a Cosmic Expedition, a thrilling and satisfying journey of the Aquarian Age, and to explore my true spiritual Self by discovering my hidden inner potentials. I guess people do those sorts of things, but it is all new to me. Still, a pass-or-fail grade hangs in the balance. So I proceed.

Other than a few students getting into cars to drive home from what must have been a cosmic expedition class, I see very few people on campus. The bookstore sign says it's open, so I enter. To my great delight I find someone inside, an attractive young lady about twenty years old. I can't help noticing her attire. If not for the large crystals hanging from her ears and necklace, she could be mistaken for a 1970s hippy-era lovechild named Daisy.

"Can I help you find something?" she inquires.

"Well, actually, I was wondering whether you might be willing to help me with a class assignment." Not her usual customer request. "You see, I am a seminary student studying various religious perspectives. I was hoping to interview someone from Astara to learn more about your beliefs."

A slow day—she is willing to give me time. We sit near the cash register and begin the interview. I have several pre-planned questions on my pad.

1. How would you describe God?

2. Who is Jesus?
3. What is wrong with our world?
4. How do we find salvation?

I explain my answer to each question before asking for hers in order to set up comparison and contrast. Her answers reveal a clear difference.

1. God is not a personal, loving father. He/She/It is the cosmic oneness we all inhabit.
2. Jesus is not God in the flesh. He is one of many enlightened ones who invite us to discover our higher selves.
3. Ours is not a world of fallen, sinful men and women. Ours is a world of men and women who have forgotten their true goodness—and their true godness.
4. Salvation is not through faith in Christ. It is through higher consciousness.

In the course of our conversation, I also discover her belief in reincarnation and karma. I am caught by surprise with a few concepts I never heard before or since. Apparently there is room among the faithful for customized variation on the general themes of Astara orthodoxy. But the main ideas of her faith appear remarkably similar to those of every New Age guru I had seen on the best-seller list.

One last question, one that I consider most important, comes to mind. What, I wonder, is her hope? What does she look forward to when this life, or rather cycle of lives, comes to an end? My religion tells me I will join God in heaven for what Jesus called eternal life. What is the promise of hers?

"I will become part of the great cosmic oneness, like a drop of water being absorbed into the vast ocean." In other words, she will cease to be an individual by becoming part of something greater. No longer aware of herself, she will vanish into the vast wonder of light. Ultimate enlightenment!

I suppose that seems exciting from her point of view. Still, if I were Daisy, I would feel cheated. After a lifetime trying to discover myself, I wouldn't eagerly anticipate the complete loss of my identity into some grand "absorption." I would feel a bit like Captain Picard of *Star Trek: The Next Generation*. He and his crew resisted the Borg, a collective society that moved from one civilization to another declaring, "Resistance is futile. You will be assimilated."

And what do I get in exchange for losing track of myself? In the words of Astara founder Robert Chaney, "Calmness and serenity are constant qualities which are part of Him, and part of you." I suppose that's something.

But my assignment is not to judge. It is to learn.

Thanking Daisy for her time and for helping me better understand what she and her community believe, I leave to sort through my notes and reflect upon what I've heard.

Members of Astara see themselves, see us all, as part of God. They strive for enlightenment to achieve higher consciousness. They believe in reincarnation, so they embrace both life after death and life before birth. They embrace the law of karma, which compels them to good deeds. Put simply, they are Hindus with a touch of Buddhism.

Very little seems new about the New Age movement. While phrases like "a lodestar on the true path of the soul" may sound new and mysterious, the belief system is nothing more or less than Eastern pantheism. Pantheism teaches that God is everything and that everything is God. All of us, good and bad, are mere drops of water in the vast sea of God.

In the movie based upon an autobiographical book by Shirley MacLaine titled *Out on a Limb,* one scene depicts pantheistic understanding in a manner most viewers found troubling. MacLaine stands on the beach beside David, her spiritual mentor, who invites her to repeat several short phrases. Normally, the ocean makes us feel humbled and small, recognizing how great our Creator must be. But David doesn't coach her to shout "Great is the Lord" or "How wonderful is your handiwork" to the God of heaven. He instead asks her to repeat three simple words: "I am God!" MacClaine hesitates. "David, I can't do that." To which he responds, "See how little you think of yourself?"

With a little coaxing, she agrees to do as instructed—timidly at first. But as they repeat the phrase in unison, over and over, her conviction grows. They turn toward the ocean, its crashing waves echoing its size and majesty, and continue their mantra: "I am God! I am God!"[72]

To someone like me, the scene shouts ultimate arrogance and blasphemy. But to MacLaine and others who embrace pantheism, it paints a scene of ultimate discovery. Shirley had finally come to realize her true identity. She, like the rest of us, is part of God. Her drop of water had finally accepted its place in the ocean.

Pantheism is most notably expressed in the Hindu faith. It differs from classical polytheism, a belief in many gods common in the ancient Greek and Roman world, and from monotheism, the belief in a supreme and personal God as proclaimed by Jews, Christians, and Muslims. And like every other world religion, it tries to answer all three suspicions of the heart.

First, it suggests that we were made for more. We should not feel satisfied with our present state. Those living in the caste system of India hope their next incarnation will be the last. A leprous beggar is an untouchable, so he wants to return as a rich ruler. A rich ruler yearns to become an Avatar—like Moses, Jesus, or Buddha—

who can enlighten others. All will eventually become part of the cosmic oneness, their version of a "something more" we all ache to know.

Second, pantheism tells its followers that something is wrong. It describes us as less than we ought to be. We've forgotten our true identity. We aren't here to serve God. We are God—or at least part of him.

Finally, pantheism seeks to make things right again by reminding us of who we truly are through a process of enlightenment. But the path to enlightenment rarely comes easy. The Hindu gets there through reincarnation. Each life provides opportunity to pay off karmic debt in hopes of moving up the incarnation hierarchy. The Buddhist gets there through higher consciousness in hopes of achieving Nirvana, a kind of cross between going to heaven and getting high on drugs.

I find little in pantheism with which I can agree. My faith starts with a very different definition of God. My God is a person; theirs is a life force. My God created the world; theirs is the world. Since how we define God dictates how we define all other subpoints, I cannot align our beliefs on matters such as who I am or what needs to be fixed. But we are trying to pick the same lock. Just like me, they want a big God. They want to feel small when contemplating ultimate reality. And they want to know life is about more than we see.

I find it interesting that even those who claim to be God expect him to be more. Shirley MacLaine shouted in front of mighty waves, not a trickling faucet. Her drop, like mine, longs for the ocean. And we both hope he is infinitely greater than ourselves.

INKLING

GOD IS MUCH MORE THAN ME.

CHAPTER TWENTY-THREE

Love Thy Enemy

Our God and your God is one and the same.

THE KORAN

I was a high school sophomore when I first noticed a billion people. Of course, at the time I didn't realize there were a billion. I thought a relatively few of them lived somewhere in the Middle East. And like most Americans, my first impressions were not good. Nor were my second, third, or fourth.

On November 4, 1979, Iranian militants stormed the United States Embassy in Tehran and took hostage about seventy Americans. Over the next 444 days, news programs presented shocking images of fellow American citizens terrorized beneath blindfolds. From what I could decipher, someone named Ayatollah Khomeini lay behind the turmoil. He was some sort of Islamic religious and political leader who had a bone to pick with America. I will never forget the images of burning flags and gun-waving Iranians cheering Allah while cursing us. Comfortably ignorant of their problems or beliefs, I knew only one thing for sure: I didn't like Muslims.

My second impression came a decade later when a man named Salman Rushdie published a book titled *The Satanic Verses*. It apparently made fun of the prophet Muhammad, prompting violent protests from Muslims in Islamabad, Pakistan, and eventually causing the very same Ayatollah to call upon "all zealous Muslims quickly to execute" both author and publisher. I remember hearing the news of how Rushdie fled into hiding while pundits debated freedom of speech and blasphemy. Unfamiliar with Islam, I had no interest in reading the book. But I wondered how a seemingly harmless English novelist could create such a stir in the Muslim world. Did they feel so devoted to Muhammad that they would murder a man over what seemed a minor offense? My second impression delivered a clear message: "If you value your life, don't mess with Islamic dogma!"

My third and fourth impressions of Islam, like the first and second, came from television news. Years of images of Israeli conflict with Palestinian terrorists under the direction of Yasser Arafat served as a constant reminder of how much Muslims hate the Jewish people. And then there was that fateful morning in September of 2001 when billowing smoke and crumbling buildings woke me to the realization of a billion people in the Islamic world—a good portion of whom would prefer me dead. Osama bin Ladin, a name I had no reason to know or desire to know, suddenly forced its way into the forefront of my vocabulary. Along with most Americans, his name slipped into that spot in our minds reserved for previous occupants—such as Adolf Hitler during World War II or Nikita Khrushchev during the Cuban Missile Crisis—previously meaningless but suddenly hated. Suddenly feared.

I realize it was unfair to characterize all Muslims by the actions of these few. After all, I wouldn't want my faith judged by the actions of a few fanatics who justify their actions in the name of Jesus—like Jim Jones or David Koresh. But like many in the West, I knew only what I saw on the news. I feel embarrassed to admit that I never read the Koran until shortly after 9–11. Despite its status as a dominant world religion, I never gave Islam much attention until my nation was at war with its faithful. And since Jesus said I am supposed to love my enemies, I figured it was time to get to know something about them.

What I discovered surprised me. To start, I didn't expect to find the Koran (or more properly, Quran) such a poetic work. It reads very much like the book of Psalms in my own Bible. And, I am told, it sounds even more beautiful in the original language. Nor did I expect it to contain variant versions of stories that I knew from Jewish and Christian Scriptures. Diving a bit deeper into the history and substance of Islam helped me understand that all three faiths share a common link.

Six centuries after the birth of Jesus Christ, an Arab businessman named Muhammad bin Abdallah gave birth to a religion while living in the city of Mecca. He didn't think of it as a new religion. In fact, Muhammad admired Judaism and Christianity, which he assumed belonged to the same faith. He saw them as far more sophisticated than the pagan traditions of his own people. He, like many Arabs, felt left out of the divine plan because God had not given them a prophet or provided a Scripture in their own language. So, while on a prayer and fasting retreat on the outskirts of Mecca, Muhammad bin Abdallah said he had an encounter with an overpowering presence and received a revelation—the first words of what would become the Koran. Two years later, he began preaching and converting fellow Arabs, who felt pleased finally to be invited to the party.

Muhammad did not try to convert Jews or Christians.[73] He had no need. From his perspective, they already had valid prophets (Moses and Jesus) and sacred texts. It was the Arabs, many of whom continued to believe in multiple smaller gods, who needed introduction to the One God whom Jews and Christians worshiped. They also needed to mend their ways, as commercial success had caused many of his tribe to neglect social justice. Through this new sect—eventually called *Islam* (meaning "surrender"), and its sacred text, the *Koran* (meaning "recitation")—Abdallah called his people to submit their entire being to *Allah* (meaning "the God") and his demand that they treat one another with justice, equity, and compassion.

Again, Muhammad did not consider his teachings as anything revolutionary. The Koran describes its message as a reminder of truths others already knew, and its God as the same supreme deity others already served.

> Do not argue with the followers of earlier revelation otherwise than in a most kindly manner—unless it be such of them as are bent on evil-doing—and say: "We believe in that which has been bestowed from on high upon us, as well as that which has been bestowed upon you; for our God and your God is one and the same, and it is unto Him that we [all] surrender ourselves." (25:4–7)

One of Muhammad's most profound realizations came more than a decade after he received his initial revelation. Arabs, he learned, were not orphaned children outside God's plan; they were the children of Abraham through the line of Ishmael. And like the children of Israel, they had a promise of God to become a great people. Tradition even suggested that Abraham had worshiped with Ishmael in the city of Mecca. So Islam was not a new faith, but the rediscovery of Arab roots, a realization of their validity before God.

After years of being ignored or resisted by Jews, Christians, and fellow Arabs alike, Muhammad did something shocking. During a public prayer in 624, he turned his face toward Mecca rather than Jerusalem—a powerful symbolic declaration. Those who prayed toward Jerusalem did so in rejection of the old pagan religions in favor of the belief in one God. By praying toward Mecca, Muhammad proclaimed Islam as something more than Judaism's black-sheep relative. He declared it the pure monotheism of

Abraham, who predates either Moses or Jesus. In the words of the Koran,

> Behold, my Sustainer has guided me to a straight way through an ever-true faith—in the way of Abraham, who turned away from all that is false, and was not of those who ascribe divinity to aught beside Him. (6:159–162)

My investigation led me to see the Muslim faith in an entirely new light. Its faithful, like Jews and Christians, claim a link to Abraham, the father of monotheism. As it turns out, those I perceived to be violent, hate-filled radicals—those billion enemies I am supposed to love—are actually my religious cousins!

~~~

I have moved from fearing to better understanding the Muslim faith—at least its original form. Like Christianity, Islam has been influenced and smeared by centuries of misinterpretation, mishandling, and mischief in its name. Not that violence is entirely foreign to its history. In fact, Muhammad himself assembled and led an army to defend and spread his message, partially in self-defense. But his early intentions suggest a sincere desire to worship the one true God. Muhammad seems to have been trying to help a deceived and disenfranchised people abandon their wayward ways and humbly serve their Maker.

Muslims claim to worship the same God as me. With the exception of certain radical sects that encourage their children to become suicide bombers and jihad militants, most Muslims teach their kids values similar to those I want mine to embrace—like self-discipline, honesty, and compassion for the poor. And while profound differences exist between the beliefs, points of similarity also appear.

First, Muslims agree that we are made for more. One of the central tenets of Islamic faith is belief in an afterlife. It talks about future judgment, when Allah will determine who will enter "the paradise of the garden" (heaven), with all of its sensual and sexual pleasure, including beautiful virgins for men. Those who do not enter paradise are sent to the fire (hell), a place reserved for idolaters, unbelievers, and the unrepentant. Muslims often use the phrase "if Allah wills" because much of Islam is predicated upon predestination, the idea that God is sovereign and that the story in which we live is being written by the Almighty Author of life. Our present lives and eternal futures, therefore, are about more than what we see.

Second, Islam teaches that something is wrong. While Muslims do not believe in the Christian doctrine of original sin, they do see man as separated from God due to ignorance and weakness. Much of Muhammad's original motive arose over concern regarding the greed and injustice of his people and his desire to reconnect them with the true God and right living.

Finally, Islam agrees that things should be made right again. In fact, Muslims have one of the most rigidly clear "to do" lists for right living of any religious group, as expressed in the five duties of all good Muslims.

Duty One: Publicly repeat the Shahada: "There is no god but Allah and Muhammad is the prophet of Allah."

Duty Two: Pray five times a day, kneeling and bowing in the prescribed manner in the direction of Mecca.

Duty Three: Give 2.5 percent of your profit to widows, orphans, the sick, or some other disadvantaged people.

Duty Four: Fast during daylight hours for the entire month of Ramadan.

Duty Five: You or your representative must make at least one pilgrimage to Mecca during your lifetime.[74]

As it turns out, my "list" looks quite different from that of Muslims. They emphasize what man must do to please God; mine celebrates what God has done to redeem man. The Koran says we are traveling different paths toward the same God. But it seems to me that their God has a very different personality than the one I serve and inspires very different religious behaviors. Still, our common, unspoken creed seeks answers to the same basic questions.

INKLING

THERE IS ONLY ONE GOD.

CHAPTER TWENTY-FOUR

To Life!

Judaism is not the problem.
Life is the problem. Judaism is the answer.

RABBI HAROLD KUSHNER

The Jews are God's uniquely chosen people. That's what my Sunday school teachers told me. That's what I continue to believe. And while I'm sure being chosen by God is quite an honor, I don't think I would want to be in their shoes.

I have always loved the Jewish people, faith, and culture—the people because I was taught that God has a special place in his heart for the Jews; the faith because it is the prologue to my own; and the culture because of what it has created through the centuries. I remember first feeling captivated by the complexity and diversity of the Jewish community years ago while reading *The Chosen* by Chaim Potok, a novel that remains one of my all-time favorites. Through the story of a friendship between two Jewish boys, one from a Conservative and the other from an Orthodox family, Potok drew me into a world rich with tradition, depth, and identity. He helped me understand something of the modern Jewish experience, both good and bad.

The bad couldn't get much worse, as his people bore the brunt of anti-Semitism for thousands of years, culminating with the Holocaust. I had one of the most disturbing experiences of my life while walking through the Holocaust Memorial Museum in Washington, D.C. A cloud of silent grief overtook me that day. Oh sure, I had learned about death camps and Hitler's other horrors. But seeing thousands of discarded Jewish shoes, photos, and lives caused the reality to hit home. It felt like my first real encounter with a departed loved one. I knew my aunt had died. But it didn't sink in until I viewed her cold cadaver lying in the casket. It sent a chill down my spine. That same chill returned as I grieved the loss of millions of God's chosen.

I think the Jewish people are a bit like Frodo Baggins in *The Lord of the Rings*. The honor of being the ring bearer comes with the onerous burden of bearing the ring. Being God's chosen seems as much burden as it is blessing. A blessing because God made a covenant with Abraham and gave the Law to Moses; a burden because he expects them to honor that covenant and obey that Law. And when either expectation gets disappointed, God takes it very personally—like a spurned lover who has found his wife in bed with another man.

The Jewish Scriptures teem with stories of this cycle. God invites the Hebrews into a special relationship. He then gives them a list of dos and don'ts, including many "thou shalts" and "thou shalt nots." You should honor your parents and rest on the Sabbath. You shouldn't murder or worship idols. Since the early Jews lived among many cultures of pagan idolatry, the "other gods" thing got them into the most trouble. In fact, a good portion of the Jewish Scriptures chronicles a pattern of leaving Jehovah to worship Baal and other gods, only to be punished. Prophets like Jeremiah had the unpleasant job of calling them to task, often comparing their religious unfaithfulness to prostitution.

> "But you have lived as a prostitute with many lovers—would you now return to me?" declares the LORD. "Look up to the barren heights and see. Is there any place where you have not been rav-

ished? By the roadside you sat waiting for lovers, sat like a nomad in the desert. You have defiled the land with your prostitution and wickedness.... You have the brazen look of a prostitute; you refuse to blush with shame."[75]

But God always remained gracious, inviting them back to himself—back to life.

"'Return, faithless people,' declares the LORD, 'for I am your husband. I will choose you.'"

A large part of Jewish identity derives from exile and persecution. Exile because through most of history they have lacked a homeland. Persecution because they have not been welcome in the homes of others. The worst example, of course, occurred in the atrocities of the Holocaust. The more common pattern finds expression in the musical *Fiddler on the Roof*. Ordered to leave the Russian village they call home, a tight-knit community of Jews suddenly finds themselves refugees. One young man puts their emotion into words. "Rabbi," he asks, "we've waited all our lives for the Messiah. Wouldn't this be a good time for him to come?" Unwilling to feed their despair, the rabbi responds with a forced twinkle in his eye: "We'll have to wait for him someplace else."

One of the reasons I find Judaism so appealing is that it stares suffering and injustice straight in the eyes while refusing to blink. Case in point: Rabbi Harold Kushner. He wrote a book titled *To Life! A Celebration of Jewish Being and Thinking*. In it, he describes the Jewish faith as "a four-thousand-year-old tradition with ideas about what it means to be human and how to make the world a holy place." He says Judaism predates Buddha and Confucius and that its "notions of God and life were the sources of Christianity and Islam." He is quick to celebrate the tremendous influence his tiny slice of the human race has had on our world, such as the poetry of the Psalms, the theories of Einstein and Freud, as well as the polio vaccine and dozens of other major medical discoveries.

And while acknowledging the irrational fear and hatred that his people have endured, he says, "Judaism is not the problem. Life is the problem, and Judaism is the answer."[76]

Is being a devout Jew really as positive an experience as Kushner suggests, or is he just a "glass half full" kind of guy? After all, history has handed Jews plenty of reasons to lose heart, perhaps more than any people on the planet. So why, with the exception of a relative few, don't they? I believe in large part it is because their faith tradition embraces and celebrates life and the God who gives it. Yes, as God's chosen people they bear the burden of high expectations and spiteful enemies. Yes, they have suffered tremendous abuse at the hands of murderous foes. But like Frodo Baggins, they also carry a very important ring. It is the Jews who introduced the world to someone very special: the Author of life.

It is no easy task to summarize all of Judaism. Like Christianity and other faiths, it has evolved into many denominations and sects. Some still look for the Messiah to rescue them from a fallen, painful world. Others have abandoned hope of a literal Messiah and instead attach their redemption to the suffering they've been asked to endure. There is Orthodox Judaism, Conservative Judaism, Reformed Judaism, and several other major categories. Within each, other subgroups have their own distinctive traditions. But all of them share a common history and find meaning in two events that universally define Jewish hope and identity. The first involves a nomad named Abraham; the second, a ruler-turned-shepherd-turned-leader named Moses.

Abraham lived about six thousand years ago. If he was like most of his fellow nomads, Abraham grew up pagan, worshiping one or more of the gods common to his era. And then one day, out of the blue, God spoke to him. He told Abraham that he had decided to make him a great nation and, through him, to bless all people. He also told him that his descendants would suffer mistreatment and enslavement. In what has come to be called *the Abrahamic covenant,* God told the Jewish people that they were uniquely chosen as the channel through which blessing would come to the world.

Those reared in the church or synagogue know the story of Moses. Everyone else has probably seen the movie *The Ten Commandments.* As a result, we know the basics. God freed his people from Egyptian slavery. There were ten plagues, a stubborn pharaoh, and Charlton Heston parting the Red Sea. But to really understand Judaism, we need to watch the sequel that no one produced. The giving of the Law, only briefly touched upon in Cecil B. DeMille's film, became the defining moment of Jewish thought. It told the Jews—and by extension, the rest of us—that God did not accept anything and everything. It clearly spelled out right from wrong, both in how we live and in how we worship. In short, it told us what it means to be good and how to make things right when we are bad.

Forty years after first receiving the Law from Moses, the Jewish people finally were ready to enter the Promised Land. But because most of the original recipients had died, God commanded a second telling of the Law, recorded for posterity in a book titled Deuteronomy (which means "law again"). Toward the end of this recap, something is said that I believe encapsulates Judaism. God says to his people:

> Now what I am commanding you today is not too difficult for you or beyond your reach. . . . No, the word is very near you; it is in your mouth and in your heart so you may obey it. . . . This day I call heaven and earth as witnesses against you that I have set before you life and death, blessings and curses. Now choose life, so that you and your children may live and that you may love

the LORD your God, listen to his voice, and hold fast to him. For the LORD is your life. (30:11–20)

Cutting right to the bottom line of faith, the direct and indirect implications seem clear. God has made himself known as the giver of life. God lets us choose between the life and blessings he is or the death and curses he isn't. God wants us to listen to and love him. These concepts lay the foundation for how Judaism responds to the heart's unspoken creed.

First, by declaring that we are made for more. Judaism tells us that God made mankind in his own image and that he wants a relationship with us. That is why God made a covenant with Abraham, inviting the Jews and all people to know him. To know life.

Second, by telling us that something is wrong. A central theme of Judaism is keeping the Law of Moses, which is much more than a system of rigid restrictions. God gave the Law as a reminder of what life is supposed to be. The Law is direct revelation from God, telling us that there is a right and a wrong way to live. It is good news, describing the way of life. But it is also bad news, telling us that we fall short through sin. And because sin offends a holy God, death is the price of disobedience.

Third, by offering a plan and hope for making it right again. The Passover celebration, instituted on the night God freed the Jews from Egypt, provides an annual connection to the temple sacrifice commonly practiced until the destruction of the temple in A.D. 70. Just as Passover blood on the doorposts protected those inside from the death angel, so the blood sacrifice in the temple provided a means of atonement from the death of sin. After A.D. 70, the Jews once again found themselves scattered over the face of the earth—shifting their attention from priest to rabbi, from sacrifice to synagogue, from temple to Torah. The Law, rather than the blood offering, became the central focus of Judaism.

Today, Judaism invites the world to life by proclaiming God's expectations and desire for mankind. It tells us that purity doesn't take away pleasure but infuses it with passion. It offers the freedom a well-disciplined athlete enjoys when he can do what others never try—suggesting we can master appetite rather than serve it and rule our passions rather than be ruled by them. To the observant Jew, the Law isn't restrictive. It does not tell us to refrain from doing what we most want to do. It is freeing, inviting us to say no to what we most need to stop. To say no to sinful patterns leading to death so that we might know true life.

And life, after all, is what God is all about.

INKLING

God invites us to life.

CHAPTER TWENTY-FIVE

Unity

May they be brought to complete unity
to let the world know that you sent me.

JESUS

If I weren't already a Christian, I'm
not sure what I would make of Christianity. It must confuse observers
to try to sort out all of the denominations, doctrines, and differences
that have emerged from what is supposed to be a single religion. I
am one of us, and yet even I find it perplexing at times.

Open the Yellow Pages of any sizable city in America and you
will see what I mean. Under the "Churches" heading we offer more
assortments than a Baskin-Robbins ice-cream shop. If you start
your search at the front of the alphabet, your finger will first scan
over African Methodist Episcopal. Already you are in trouble, since
Methodist and Episcopal show up later as separate denominations.
Next comes Anglican, the church our Pilgrim forefathers came to
America to flee, then Apostolic and Assemblies of God. Moving on,
you will hit Baptist—which subdivides into at least a dozen independent and denominational varieties, including American Baptist,
Conservative Baptist, Free Will Baptist, General Baptist, Regular
Baptist, and of course, Southern Baptist, the largest Protestant
denomination in the country.

Which raises another interesting dilemma: Protestant versus Catholic. You come to Catholic under C. It includes churches with names like Saint Francis of Assisi or Our Lady of Perpetual Help, both of which bother Baptists who consider every believer a saint and who view the Catholic obsession with Mary a form of idolatry. Roman Catholics in turn consider Baptists and other Protestants wayward siblings at best, cults at worst.

Moving on down the list, you will encounter a list of Charismatic churches, which are without question our most colorful variety. You may be familiar with this style of Christianity from watching their more flamboyant representatives on television—the ones with big hair and pretentious sets. But they aren't all like that. Most are sincere believers who happen to express their emotions more emphatically than the stoic among us.

From there you can move through the remaining twenty-three letters of the alphabet to encounter a wide array of other Christian groups—from Greek Orthodox to Lutheran to Nazarene to Reformed—all claiming Jesus Christ as their ultimate head while often accusing the rest of falling somewhere outside orthodoxy. This causes us to spend an awful lot of energy trying to evangelize one another.

Doctrinal disputes fill Christian history. Sometimes the arguments have remained academic and civil. Other times they have not. Today I lovingly poke fun at friends who belong to other denominations. But at times such differences were neither loving nor fun. We even killed one another over whether we claimed loyalty to Rome or Henry VIII, burning "heretics" at the stake.

And yet, Jesus said to his followers, "All men will know that you are my disciples if you love one another." I think we've disappointed him.

Through most of history, however, Christians have acted like a boisterous family, fighting and arguing with each other over big and small matters alike—kind of an, "I can beat up my kid brother, but you best not try it!' environment. Still, I can't help wondering what those outside our walls must think of all the shouting—or what Jesus must think in light of his prayer, "May they be brought to complete unity to let the world know that you sent me."

I'm glad I became a Christian during childhood. That fact spared me the sifting and sorting process. I simply accepted the version of Christianity my parents offered. We attended an Independent Baptist church, not to be confused with Southern, Northern, American, Conservative, General, Regular, Free Will, or any of the other roughly fifty Baptist denominations. We considered all of them borderline heretics. Our brand of Christianity featured a distinct culture. My dad, who served on the deacon board, was called "Brother," as were all of the men. The highest-ranking brother was the preacher, which is what we called him, as opposed to "pastor." And when his preaching was on a roll, he expected and received a congregational "amen" to affirm the point or fill the silence. The music minister led us in hymns like "Onward Christian Soldiers," "The Old Rugged Cross," and of course, "Amazing Grace." We felt passionate about Jesus. But we maintained our composure and never raised our hands, lest we seem Charismatic.

I got "saved" (the term we used to describe conversion) when I was seven years old by repeating a prayer the preacher suggested. I later walked the aisle—probably during the fifth verse of the hymn "Just As I Am"—indicating my desire and readiness to be baptized. We didn't sprinkle; no good Baptist does. We dunked. And coming up out of the water prompted a chorus of "Amen, brother" from a crowd that considered water immersion the first and most important sign of true commitment to a lifelong walk with Jesus. Not that baptism was the same thing as being saved. We always carefully kept them distinct. I will never forget the preacher's reaction when I walked the aisle and told him I wanted to be baptized. Concerned that a seven-year-old might not fully understand, he asked, "Don't you think you should be saved first?"

"I already am!" came my indignant reply, offended that he would think I had missed a step in the process. Salvation must precede baptism—a point made quite clear even to my immature understanding.

Ours was not a highly educated congregation. Made up mostly of blue-collar workers, we figured if the preacher said it, it must be true. We got strict about small matters like music and hair styles, and almost fanatical with nonessential matters like the King James Bible and prophecy. For the most part, however, we remained harmless to everyone but ourselves.

As an adult, I walked away from that subculture. Like many reared in a fundamentalist or legalistic church environment, I developed a bit of an attitude, blaming it for problems I just as likely would have had anyway. I saw myself as too sophisticated for its simplicity. But the older I get, the more profound that simple faith becomes. I wasn't taught to respect the depth and complexity of Christian thought and tradition or the rich tapestry of variety the church offers. I did, however, learn that I was a sinner who needed to be saved—a message, by the way, all Christians embrace in one form or another.

∽☙∾

How can a single belief fit so many cultures, styles, quirks, and socioeconomic groups? What at the core of the Christian faith makes it appealing to so many with so little in common? What essential ideas unite such diversity, and how do those ideas differ from other world religions?

The best way to answer such questions is to examine how Christianity responds to the heart's unspoken creed.

First, Christianity tells us we were made in the very image of God. "So God created man in his own image, in the image of God he created him; male and female he created them." Humans were given dominion over everything on earth. We were made for intimacy with the Almighty, walking hand in hand with him "in the cool of the day" (Genesis 3:8), like a beloved child or a cherished bride. I've often wondered what it must have been like to enjoy the sights, sounds, smells, and tastes of a virgin world. What must Eden have been like? It was a place of beauty unlike any we can comprehend, perfectly designed for its inhabitants to enjoy the most satisfying, healthy, adventurous, and pleasure-filled lives possible. It probably had the sandy beaches of a tropical paradise, the breathtaking majesty of the Rocky Mountains, the crashing waves of the Oregon coast, the fresh breeze of an eastern seaport, and the sweet aroma of a Midwestern apple farm.

As originally created, we were innocent beings. Everything in existence was good, a gift from the heart and hand of a good God. Adam, Eve, and their descendants had so much to look forward to! From tasting their first mixed-fruit drink to orbiting earth in a space shuttle, a whole world of discovery, invention, and adventure waited to be enjoyed.

But something went wrong—the second truth of Christian faith. "For all have sinned and fall short of the glory of God."[77] The good God was rejected. Adam, our father and representative, chose to join a rebellion launched by Lucifer in which those created removed themselves from God's protective rule. As a result, we live in a world dominated by the opposite of good. Beauty gave way to ugliness, justice to cruelty, joy to sorrow, life to death. According to Christianity, God did not invent evil. Suffering and pain are not devices within the divine torture chamber, used on those who refuse to obey heaven's edicts. Rather, they're the result of living in a world flawed by rebellion against goodness. And they never were supposed to be part of our lives.

Finally, Christianity answers tenet three of the heart's creed. The "something wrong" must be made right again. "But God demonstrates his own love for us in this: While we were still sinners, Christ died for us" (Romans 5:8). Christianity offers a solution unlike any other religion. Every other faith tells me I must get my act together if I hope to reach God. I must either obey commandments, expand awareness, pay off karmic debt, or become a better person. But Christianity is not about what I do; it is about what God did. He replaced my despair with hope by becoming the hero of life's drama. He paid the penalty for my sin and rebellion in order to redeem me back to himself.

God did not remain in heaven and bark orders or criticize our inadequate efforts to reach him. Instead he took the initiative to reach us. According to Christianity, the author entered the story. God became man so that man could know God.

I've seen the best and worst Christianity has to offer. At times in my life I have grown angry at what I've seen, from silly legalistic rules to serious hypocrisy. Like other Christians, I feel embarrassed by portions of our history—as when the Church silenced Galileo and killed Muslims. I recognize such incidents as anomalies. The history of every faith has moments it would rather forget, when those who proclaim its creed ignore its message. I also realize such failures reflect a truth my faith proclaims: we are an imperfect, fallen race. Still, they make me angry.

Despite feeling embarrassed by some Christians, I've always remained amazed by Christ. And at the core, Christianity is about Christ. Who he is. What he's done. How his life, death, and resurrection answer the unspoken yearning of my heart—and resolve the dissonant chord of my life.

Every religion reminds me that I am made for more. Every religion reaches for God. Every religion offers to make the wrong right again. But only one religion, Christianity, is honest enough to tell me that I can't solve my own problem. I can't obey enough rules, offer enough sacrifices, or become enlightened enough to rise above the wretchedness around and within me. All I can do is humbly accept the redemption offered by the One who made me for more and who heroically sacrificed himself on my behalf. It's like the preacher told me when I was seven. I am a sinner who needs to be saved.

INKLING

It is God who makes the wrong right again.

Conclusion: The Right Key

*I believe in Christianity as I believe that the Sun has risen,
not only because I see it, but because by it I see everything else.*

C. S. Lewis

Before May 10, 1985, I considered myself a fairly open-minded guy. Since then I have become narrow-minded and biased, limiting myself to one possibility out of many. You see, on that day, I got married. And saying "I do" to one woman meant saying "I don't" to the rest. That doesn't mean I hate all other women—but it does mean they ceased to be options for me.

The same thing happened when I embraced Christianity as truth. Accepting one meant rejecting others. When we pick and choose from various religious traditions, we do not show our broad-mindedness or inclusivity. We are more like the man who sleeps with multiple women. He doesn't take sexual intimacy seriously. Rather than sacred, he sees sex as a game.

Religion is like marriage. It is by definition exclusive. That doesn't mean a religious person hates all other faiths or even views them as entirely wrong. But we can't view them as equally right. The creed of each excludes the creed of others. Jesus certainly did so when he rejected the notion that all paths lead to God. "Enter through the narrow gate. For wide is the gate and broad is the road that leads to destruction, and many enter through it. But small is the gate and narrow the road that leads to life, and only a few find it" (Matthew 7:13).

Jesus clearly claimed exclusivity. "I am the way and the truth and the life. No one comes to the Father except through me" (John 14:6).

But Jesus also made his offer available to everyone . . . "For God so loved the world that he gave his one and only Son, that whoever believes in him shall not perish but have eternal life. For God did not send his Son into the world to condemn the world, but to save the world through him" (John 3:16–17).

I believe every person is on a spiritual journey, seeking the truth. But for some, the journey seems more like aimless wandering— never reaching the intended destination. Every quest should have a prize. Every search is supposed to find. While I believe all religions reach for the same God, Jesus said they don't all find him. On one level, I don't want to hear that. On another level, I know it's true. It must be. If we believe in everything, we believe in nothing. Jesus is either who he claimed or he's an arrogant liar. He died paying for my sins, or he died getting what he deserved. As a Christian, I believe Jesus' claim to be the intended destination of every spiritual quest. He is the prize pursued, the truth sought.

I became a Christian in large part because my parents were Christians. I remain a Christian for a million other reasons, some of which I've tried to share in this book—inklings of God I have encountered outside the walls of formal religion that have led me to see Christianity as the one faith capable of confirming what my heart suspects. Like peering through the lenses of a proper eyeglass prescription, it brings a blurry world into clear focus.

Of course, it is possible that I believe Christianity to be true because I want it to be true—the wishful thinking of a needy man. Perhaps. But desire does not undermine discovery. Hunger points us to food. Our hearts should yearn for that which it most needs. I can't ignore the three suspicions of my heart. Nor can you.

> We know we are made for more. Christianity tells me I am made in the image of my Maker.
>
> We know something is wrong. Christianity says I live in a fallen world.
>
> We know it needs to be set right again. Christianity tells me God is my redeemer.

In short, Christianity opens the lock. I must agree with two men who once rejected the Christian faith but later became some of its most articulate spokesmen. Why do millions of us embrace Christianity? C. S. Lewis said it well: "I believe in Christianity like I believe that the sun has risen, not only because I see it, but because by it I see everything else"[78]

G. K. Chesterton said it even better: "Because it fits the lock; because it is like life. It is one among many stories; only it happens to be a true story. It is one among many philosophies; only it happens to be the truth. We accept it; and the ground is solid under our feet and the road is open before us."[79]

The road is open before us. Christians do not need to live a closed-minded life. God may not be in all things, but he can and does speak through all things. The atheist has to see most of the world as mad or delusional. The Christian, on the other hand, is free to hold a more liberal view—to see others as partly right because they've picked up bits and pieces of truth that resonate with the heart, pointing them to a God who fits the lock.

A God of goodness and beauty who judges evil and cruelty.

A God of life and light who overcomes death and darkness.

A God of creativity and order who makes all things beautiful.

A God who is both author and hero of the story we inhabit.

A God who, try as we might, is impossible to avoid.

Notes

1. Frank McCourt, "God in America," *Life* magazine (December 1998), 63–64.
2. Romans 1:19–20 NLT.
3. Romans 1:21 NLT.
4. J. R. R. Tolkien, *The Tolkien Reader* (New York: Ballantine Books, 1966), 79.
5. C. S. Lewis, *Mere Christianity* (New York: Simon & Schuster, 1996), 121.
6. *Into the Arms of Strangers: Stories of the Kindertransport*, Deborah Oppenheimer, producer; Mark Jonathan Harris, writer/director.
7. Leo Tolstoy, *War and Peace* (New York: Barnes & Noble, 1993), 593.
8. Leo Tolstoy, *A Confession* (New York: Penguin Books, 1987), 65.
9. C. S. Lewis, *The Screwtape Letters* (New York: Bantam Books, 1982), 26.
10. Ian Buruma, *Diana, Princess of Wales*, *Time* magazine, Online Archive.
11. Bharati Mukherjee, *Mother Teresa*, *Time* magazine, Online Archive.
12. Ibid.
13. St. Thomas Aquinas, *The Pocket Aquinas* (New York: Pocket Books, 1960), 269.
14. Matthew 6:9–13 KJV.
15. Mark Twain, *Letters from the Earth* (New York: HarperPerennial, 1991), 27.
16. Ibid., 49.
17. Dorothy L. Sayers, *The Devil to Pay* (London: Victor Gollancz, 1939), 29.
18. Ibid., 106.

19. Dan Barker, *Dear Christian* (Nontract No. 1, Dan Barker/FFRF, 1987).

20. Ibid.

21. J. Budziszewski, *The Revenge of Conscience* (Dallas: Spence, 1999), xv.

22. Ibid., xiii.

23. Ibid., xvi.

24. Harold Kushner, *When Bad Things Happen to Good People* (New York: Avon, 1981), 148.

25. Neale Donald Walsch, *Conversations with God* (New York: G.P. Putnam, 1996), 36.

26. Ibid., 61.

27. Leo Tolstoy, *The Death of Ivan Ilyich* (New York: Bantam, 1981), 102–105.

28. Stephen W. Hawking, *A Brief History of Time* (New York: Bantam, 1988), 127, 174–75.

29. Francis Crick, *Unlocking the Mystery of Life* video (Illustra Media, 2002).

30. Hugh Ross, *The Fingerprint of God* (Orange, Calif.: Promise, 1989).

31. *The Dialogues of Plato* (New York: Bantam, 1986), 7.

32. Ibid., 8.

33. J. R. R. Tolkien, *The Silmarillion* (Boston: Houghton-Mifflin, 1977), 15–16.

34. Ibid.

35. Ibid.

36. G. K. Chesterton, *The Everlasting Man* (San Francisco: Ignatius, 1925), 30–35.

37. Ibid.

38. Francis Schaeffer, *The God Who Is There* (Winchester, Ill.: Crossway, 1982), 28.

39. George MacDonald, *Lilith,* chapter 3.

40. Peter Kreeft, *Christianity for Modern Pagans* (San Francisco: Ignatius, 1993), 51.

41. Christopher Reeve, "Searching for God," *Rosie* magazine (October 2002).

42. Ibid.

43. G. K. Chesterton, *Saint Francis of Assisi* (New York: Image Doubleday, 2001).

44. Andrew Carroll, *War Letters* (New York: Scribners, 2001), 144.
45. Fyodor Dostoyevsky, *The Brothers Karamazov* (New York: Vintage, 1991), 267.
46. Ibid.
47. Theodore Dalrymple, *Life at the Bottom* (Chicago: Ivan R. Dee, 2001), 5.
48. Budziszewski, *Revenge*, 5.
49. Dostoyevsky, *Brothers Karamazov*, 632.
50. William Golding, *Lord of the Flies* (New York: Wideview/Perigee Books: 1954), 184.
51. Romans 7:15–17 NLT.
52. Charles Dickens, *Christmas Books of Charles Dickens* (New York: Black's Readers Service), 6–7.
53. Ibid., 30.
54. Ibid., 92–99.
55. Ibid., 6–7.
56. Ibid., 30.
57. Ibid., 92–99
58. Ibid.
59. Ibid.
60. Victor Hugo, *Les Miserables* (New York: Modern Library, 1992), 67.
61. Ibid., 92.
62. Ibid., 69.
63. *Contact*, film, Robert Zemeckis, director (Warner Studios, 1997).
64. Jeremiah Creedon, "God with a Million Faces," *Utne Reader* (August 1998), 42–44.
65. McCourt, "God in America," 63–64.
66. Edward Gibbon, *The Decline and Fall of the Roman Empire* (New York: Penguin, 1980), xx.
67. Chesterton, *Everlasting Man*, 108.
68. Gibbon, *Decline and Fall*, 262–70.
69. Chesterton, *Everlasting Man*, 110.
70. Ibid., 248.
71. *www.astara.org*.
72. *Out on a Limb*, film, Robert Butler, director (Anchor Bay Entertainment, 1987).
73. Karen Armstrong, *Islam: A Short History* (New York: Modern Library, 2000).

74. Fritz Ridenour, *So What's The Difference?* (Ventura, Calif.: Regal, 2001), 75–87.

75. Jeremiah 3:1–3.

76. Harold Kushner, *To Life! A Celebration of Jewish Being and Thinking* (Boston: Little, Brown, 1993), 4.

77. Roman 3:23.

78. C. S. Lewis, *The Weight of Glory* (San Francisco: HarperCollins, 2001), 140.

79. Chesterton, *Everlasting Man,* 249.

Author Contact Information

If you are interested in contacting Kurt Bruner for a speaking engagement or any other purpose, send an email to . . . *InklingsofGod@aol.com*